CONTENTS

HOW TO USE THIS GUIDE

SCOPE AND SEQUENCE

The story of the Bible reveals that heaven and earth are woven more closely together than we might think. All through the Bible, we find two parallel and beautiful dramas unfolding.

There is the **lower story**. Humans live on earth and see things from a horizontal perspective. We can't see what is around the bend but must make decisions on which way to go, where we will live, and how we will respond to what happens to us. We focus on getting through the day as best we can. We interpret why we think other people do what they do. We struggle to know why certain things happen and why other things don't happen.

Then there is the **upper story**. This is how the story is unfolding from God's perspective. Heaven is breaking into our world, and the story of God's seeking love, perpetual grace, and longing for a relationship with ordinary people is breathtaking. Of course, as humans living on this earth, we won't always be able see what is taking place in this upper story. But we can be sure that God is always present, at work, and active in every detail of our lives.

The objective of *God the Creator*—the first in a series of three small-group studies in The Story series—is to introduce you to these lower and upper stories. In this study, you will look at how God created the world and walked with his first children in a beautiful garden before sin destroyed that harmonious relationship. You will see how God called Abraham to build a nation, how Joseph saved his people from famine, how Moses led the people out of slavery, and how Joshua led them to conquer the promised land. You will explore the story of the judges and close with a look at a woman named Ruth—from whom would come the Messiah.

God wants to be with you. He wants to fill your life with greater purpose, meaning, and understanding. He wants to weave your lower story into his greater upper story that he has been writing. He wants to walk with you in every situation of life. As you recognize how closely his story and your story fit together, you *will* experience his love, grace, and wisdom.

SESSION OUTLINE

Each session is divided into two parts. In the group section, you will watch a video teaching from Randy Frazee and follow along with the outline that has been provided. (Note that you can watch these videos via streaming access at any time by following the instructions found on the inside front cover of this guide.) You will then recite the key verse(s), the key idea, and engage in some guided group discussion through the questions provided. You will close your group with a brief time of prayer.

PERSONAL STUDY

At the end of the group section, you will find a series of readings and study questions for you to go through on your own during the week. The first section will help you *know the story* by asking you to read several key passages from the Bible that were covered during your group time. The next section will help you *understand the story* through a short reading from Randy Frazee that will help you grasp the main takeaways. The third section will help you *live the story* by challenging you to put what you have learned into practice. The final section will help you *tell the story* through a short prompt for a conversation starter around a meal or dinner table. **The personal study is a critical component in helping you grasp the overall story of the Bible, so be sure to complete this study during the week before your next group meeting.**

GROUP SIZE

God the Creator can be experienced in a group setting (such as a Bible study, Sunday school class, or small-group gathering) and also as an individual study. If you are doing the study as a group with a large number of participants, it is recommended that everyone watches the video together and then breaks up into smaller groups of four to six for the discussion time. In either case, you can access the teaching videos via the streaming code found on the inside front cover.

MATERIALS NEEDED

Each participant in the group should have his or her own study guide. Although the course can be fully experienced with just the video and study guide, participants are also encouraged to have a copy of *The Story*, which includes selections from the *New International Version* that relate to each week's session.

Reading *The Story* as you go through the study will provide even deeper insights and make the journey even richer and more meaningful.

FACILITATION

Each group should appoint a facilitator who is responsible for keeping track of time during discussions and activities. Facilitators may also read questions aloud and monitor discussions, prompting participants to respond and ensuring everyone that has the opportunity to participate. (For more thorough instructions, refer to the the leader's guide that is included at the back of this guide.)

TIMELINE OF *THE STORY*

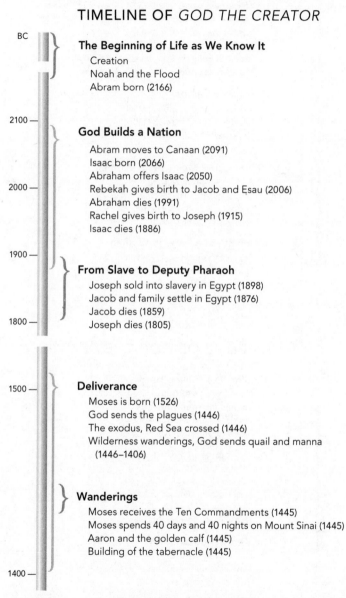

TIMELINE OF *GOD THE CREATOR*

BC

The Beginning of Life as We Know It
Creation
Noah and the Flood
Abram born (2166)

2100 —

God Builds a Nation
Abram moves to Canaan (2091)
Isaac born (2066)
Abraham offers Isaac (2050)
Rebekah gives birth to Jacob and Esau (2006)
2000 —
Abraham dies (1991)
Rachel gives birth to Joseph (1915)
Isaac dies (1886)

1900 —

From Slave to Deputy Pharaoh
Joseph sold into slavery in Egypt (1898)
Jacob and family settle in Egypt (1876)
Jacob dies (1859)
1800 —
Joseph dies (1805)

1500 —

Deliverance
Moses is born (1526)
God sends the plagues (1446)
The exodus, Red Sea crossed (1446)
Wilderness wanderings, God sends quail and manna
(1446–1406)

Wanderings
Moses receives the Ten Commandments (1445)
Moses spends 40 days and 40 nights on Mount Sinai (1445)
Aaron and the golden calf (1445)
Building of the tabernacle (1445)

1400 —

Note: Dates are approximate and dependent on the interpretative theories of various scholars.

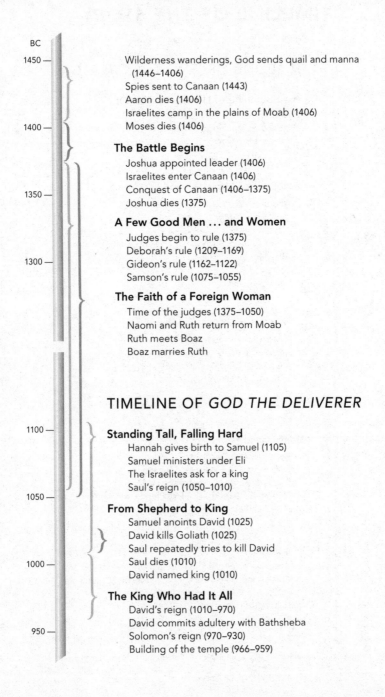

BC

1450 —

Wilderness wanderings, God sends quail and manna
    (1446–1406)
Spies sent to Canaan (1443)
Aaron dies (1406)
Israelites camp in the plains of Moab (1406)

1400 —

Moses dies (1406)

The Battle Begins

Joshua appointed leader (1406)
Israelites enter Canaan (1406)
Conquest of Canaan (1406–1375)

1350 —

Joshua dies (1375)

A Few Good Men ... and Women

Judges begin to rule (1375)
Deborah's rule (1209–1169)

1300 —

Gideon's rule (1162–1122)
Samson's rule (1075–1055)

The Faith of a Foreign Woman

Time of the judges (1375–1050)
Naomi and Ruth return from Moab
Ruth meets Boaz
Boaz marries Ruth

TIMELINE OF *GOD THE DELIVERER*

1100 —

Standing Tall, Falling Hard

Hannah gives birth to Samuel (1105)
Samuel ministers under Eli
The Israelites ask for a king

1050 —

Saul's reign (1050–1010)

From Shepherd to King

Samuel anoints David (1025)
David kills Goliath (1025)
Saul repeatedly tries to kill David

1000 —

Saul dies (1010)
David named king (1010)

The King Who Had It All

David's reign (1010–970)
David commits adultery with Bathsheba

950 —

Solomon's reign (970–930)
Building of the temple (966–959)

BC

1000—

David dies (970)
Solomon's reign (970–930)
Solomon displays great wisdom
950— Building of the temple (966–959)
Solomon marries foreign wives and betrays God

900—

A Kingdom Torn in Two

Division of the kingdom (930)
King Jeroboam I of Israel reigns (930–909)
King Rehoboam of Judah reigns (930–913)
850— King Ahab of Israel reigns (874–853)
King Jehoshaphat of Judah (872–848)

Elijah's ministry in Israel (875–848)
Elisha's ministry in Israel (c. 848–797)
800— Amos's ministry in Israel (760–750)
Hosea's ministry in Israel (750–715)

750—

The Kingdoms Fall

Fall of Israel (722)
700— Exile of Israel to Assyria (722)
Isaiah's ministry in Judah (740–681)
Hezekiah's reign (715–686)

Manasseh's reign (697–642)
650— Amon's reign (642–640)
Josiah's reign (640–609)
Jeremiah's ministry in Judah (626–585)
Jehoiakim's reign (609–598)
Zedekiah's reign (597–586)
600— Ezekiel's ministry (593–571)
Fall of Jerusalem (586)

A Prophet in Exile

550— Daniel exiled to Babylon (605)
Daniel's ministry (605–536)
Nebuchadnezzar's reign (605–562)
Daniel and the lions' den (539)
500— Fall of Babylon (539)

BC

550—

The Return Home

First return of exiles to Jerusalem (538)
Ministries of Haggai and Zechariah (520–480)
Exiles face opposition in building the temple
Temple restoration completed (516)

500—

The Queen of Beauty and Courage

Xerxes' reign in Persia (486–465)
Esther becomes queen of Persia (479)

450—

Esther saves the Jews from Haman's murderous plot
Days of Purim are established

Second return of exiles to Jerusalem under Ezra (458)
Last group of exiles return to Jerusalem under Nehemiah (445)

400—

Exiles face opposition in rebuilding the wall
Jerusalem's wall rebuilt (445)
Malachi's ministry (c. 440–430)

10 —

TIMELINE OF *GOD THE SAVIOR*

5 BC —

Jesus' Birth and Ministry

Mary gives birth to Jesus the Messiah (6/5)
Joseph, Mary, and Jesus' flight to Egypt (5/4)

5 AD —

Jesus' visit to the temple (AD 7/8)

10 —

15 —

John the Baptist begins ministry (26)
Jesus baptized (26)
Jesus begins ministry (26)

20 —

Jesus uses parables to teach (26)
Wedding at Cana (27)
The woman at the well (27)
John the Baptist imprisoned (27/28)

25 —

Jesus gives Sermon on the Mount (28)
Jesus sends closest followers out to preach (28)
John the Baptist dies (28/29)

30 —

Jesus feeds 5,000 people (29)
Jesus proclaims himself as the bread of life (29)

AD
25—

Jesus, the Son of God
Jesus teaches at the Mount of Olives (29)
Jesus resurrects Lazarus (29)
Jesus drives the money changers from the temple (30)
Judas betrays Jesus (30)

30—

The Hour of Darkness
The Lord's Supper (30)
Jesus washes his disciples' feet
Jesus comforts his disciples
Jesus is arrested
Peter denies Jesus
Jesus is crucified

35—

40—

The Resurrection
Jesus is buried (30)
Jesus is resurrected
Jesus appears to Mary Magdalene and the disciples

45—

New Beginnings
Jesus' ascension (30)
Coming of the Holy Spirit at Pentecost
Paul believed in Jesus as the promised Messiah (35)
James martyred, Peter imprisoned (44)
Paul's first missionary journey (46–48)

50—

55—

Paul's Mission
Paul's first missionary journey (46–48)
Jerusalem Council (49–50)
Paul's second missionary journey (50–52)
Paul's third missionary journey (53–57)

60—

Paul's Final Days
Paul's first imprisonment in Rome (59–62)
Paul's second imprisonment in Rome and execution (67–68)
John exiled on Patmos (90–95)

65—

70—

The End of Time
John becomes a disciple (26)
John exiled on Patmos (90–95)
Revelation written (95)

90—

95—

THE BEGINNING OF LIFE AS WE KNOW IT

GENESIS 1–11

WELCOME

The story of the Bible begins with a "big bang." In the opening pages of Genesis, we read that the Spirit of God was hovering over a place that was formless, empty, and dark. But then God initiated the spark that would lead to the creation of our world . . . and our universe. This big bang was no accident. God was *intentional* in creating the heavens, the earth, and all the amazing things that are contained within them. But the *real* point of Genesis is even more amazing: God created this place *to be with us*. He no longer wanted only to enjoy the perfect community he had as the Trinity (Father, Son, Holy Spirit). The Ultimate Author of this grand story wanted to share it with us. "In the beginning" God came up with a plan to perfectly connect his upper story with our lower story. He literally desired to bring heaven down to earth—first to create a paradise, then to create people in his own image, and then to come down and do life with us. Perfectly. Just as he had experienced perfect oneness as Father, Son, and Holy Spirit.

VIDEO TEACHING NOTES

Welcome to session one of *God the Creator*. If this is your first time meeting together as a group, take a few moments to introduce yourselves. Watch the video (see the streaming video access provided on the inside front cover) and use the following outline to record some of the main points. The answer key is found at the end of the session.

- God wants us to read the Bible like we gaze at a _____—a tapestry of individual stories that shout out a _____ message from God.

- The point of the _____, the purpose of the creation, the pride and joy of God's _____ is revealed on the opening pages. What is the apple of God's eye? The magnum opus of his work? _____—__!

- God's grand _____ was to go on walks with his children; to be in their presence. God creates the _____ story so he can come down from the _____ story to do life with us.

- In one act of _____ _____, Adam and Eve rejected God's vision in exchange for a vision to be _____ _____ _____.

- Living with a _____ _____, with other people with a _____ _____, on an earth that is _____, is not the vision of life that God had in mind.

- The choice of Adam and the sin nature banished him from the _____ of God. Every one of us are born with this sin nature, separated from a _____ with God through the choice of one man.

GETTING STARTED

Begin your discussion by reciting the key verse and key idea together as a group. Now try to state the key verse from memory. On your first attempt, use your notes if you need help. On your second attempt, try to state it completely from memory.

KEY VERSE: "So God created mankind in his own image, in the image of God he created them; male and female he created them" (Genesis 1:27).

KEY IDEA: God's vision was to come down and to be with us in a beautiful garden. But the first two people reject God's vision. Their decision introduces sin into the world and keeps humanity from experiencing community with God. The rest of the Bible is God's story of how he made it possible for us to enter back into relationship with him.

GROUP DISCUSSION

Take a few minutes with your group members to discuss what you just watched and explore these concepts in Scripture.

1. What part of this week's teaching encouraged or challenged you the most? Why?

   _____

   _____

   _____

   _____

   _____

2. What do you think it means to be created in the image of God?

   _____

   _____

   _____

   _____

   _____

3. What in the story of the garden gives you the most encouragement? Why?

   _____

   _____

   _____

   _____

   _____

4. How does the story of Cain and Abel unsettle you or challenge you?

_____

_____

_____

_____

5. What hope and promise do you find in the story of Noah?

_____

_____

_____

_____

6. What is your biggest takeaway as you reflect on what you learned this week?

_____

_____

_____

_____

CLOSING PRAYER

One of the most important things we can do together in community is to pray for each other. This is not simply a closing prayer to end your group time but a portion of time to share prayer requests and life, to review how God has answered past prayers, and to actually pray for one another. Use the space below to record prayer requests and praises. Also, make sure to pray by name for people God might add to your group—especially your neighbors.

Name   Request/Praise

_____   _____
_____   _____
_____   _____
_____   _____
_____   _____

FOR NEXT WEEK

Next week, we will look at the story of how God's covenant promise with Abraham would accomplish his upper story plan through building the nation of Israel. Before your next group meeting, be sure to read through the following personal study, complete the exercises, and memorize the key verse for the session.

VIDEO NOTES ANSWER KEY

mural, single / story, handiwork, people—us / vision, lower, upper / free will, their own gods / sin nature, sin nature, cursed / presence, relationship

PERSONAL STUDY

Every session in this guide contains a personal study to help you make meaningful connections between your life and what you are learning each week. Take some time after your group meeting each week to read through this section and complete the personal study. In total, it should take about one hour to complete. Some people like to spread it out, devoting about ten to fifteen minutes a day. Others choose one larger block of time during the week to work through it in one sitting. There is no right or wrong way to do this! Just choose a plan that best fits your needs and schedule and then allow the Scripture to take root in your heart.

KNOW THE STORY

The majority of people—even those who have attended church all their lives—view the Bible as an ancient book about what God did "in days long ago." It is amazing when we come to realize that God's upper story in the Bible connects with our own lower story of going to work, caring for our families, and trying to lead honorable lives. With this in mind, read the following key passages from *The Story*, and then answer the reflection questions that follow.

> *In the beginning God created the heavens and the earth. Now the earth was formless and empty, darkness was over the*

surface of the deep, and the Spirit of God was hovering over the waters.

And God said, "Let there be light," and there was light. God saw that the light was good, and he separated the light from the darkness. God called the light "day," and the darkness he called "night." And there was evening, and there was morning—the first day (Genesis 1:1–5).

Then God said, "Let us make mankind in our image, in our likeness, so that they may rule over the fish in the sea and the birds in the sky, over the livestock and all the wild animals, and over all the creatures that move along the ground."

*So God created mankind in his own image,
    in the image of God he created them;
    male and female he created them.*

God blessed them and said to them, "Be fruitful and increase in number; fill the earth and subdue it. Rule over the fish in the sea and the birds in the sky and over every living creature that moves on the ground."

Then God said, "I give you every seed-bearing plant on the face of the whole earth and every tree that has fruit with seed in it. They will be yours for food. And to all the beasts of the earth and all the birds in the sky and all the creatures that move along the ground—everything that has the breath of life in it—I give every green plant for food." And it was so.

God saw all that he had made, and it was very good. And there was evening, and there was morning—the sixth day (Genesis 1:26–31).

Now the serpent was more crafty than any of the wild animals the LORD *God had made. He said to the woman, "Did God really say, 'You must not eat from any tree in the garden'?"*

The woman said to the serpent, "We may eat fruit from the trees in the garden, but God did say, 'You must not eat fruit from the tree that is in the middle of the garden, and you must not touch it, or you will die'" (Genesis 3:1–3).

When the woman saw that the fruit of the tree was good for food and pleasing to the eye, and also desirable for gaining wisdom, she took some and ate it. She also gave some to her husband, who was with her, and he ate it. Then the eyes of both of them were opened, and they realized they were naked; so they sewed fig leaves together and made coverings for themselves.

Then the man and his wife heard the sound of the LORD *God as he was walking in the garden in the cool of the day, and they hid from the* LORD *God among the trees of the garden. But the* LORD *God called to the man, "Where are you?"*

He answered, "I heard you in the garden, and I was afraid because I was naked; so I hid."

And he said, "Who told you that you were naked? Have you eaten from the tree that I commanded you not to eat from?" (Genesis 3:6–11).

The LORD *God made garments of skin for Adam and his wife and clothed them. And the* LORD *God said, "The man has now become like one of us, knowing good and evil. He must not be allowed to reach out his hand and take also from the tree of life and eat, and live forever." So the* LORD *God banished him from the Garden of Eden to work the ground from which he had been taken. After he drove the man out, he placed on the east side of the Garden of Eden cherubim and a flaming sword flashing back and forth to guard the way to the tree of life* (Genesis 3:21–24).

The Lord saw how great the wickedness of the human race had become on the earth, and that every inclination of the thoughts of the human heart was only evil all the time. The Lord regretted that he had made human beings on the earth, and his heart was deeply troubled. So the Lord said, "I will wipe from the face of the earth the human race I have created—and with them the animals, the birds and the creatures that move along the ground—for I regret that I have made them." But Noah found favor in the eyes of the Lord (Genesis 6:5–8).

Then God said to Noah and to his sons with him: "I now establish my covenant with you and with your descendants after you and with every living creature that was with you— the birds, the livestock and all the wild animals, all those that came out of the ark with you—every living creature on earth. I establish my covenant with you: Never again will all life be destroyed by the waters of a flood; never again will there be a flood to destroy the earth." . . .

And God said, "This is the sign of the covenant I am making between me and you and every living creature with you, a covenant for all generations to come: I have set my rainbow in the clouds, and it will be the sign of the covenant between me and the earth.

"Whenever the rainbow appears in the clouds, I will see it and remember the everlasting covenant between God and all living creatures of every kind on the earth" (Genesis 9:8–16).

1. What authority did God give to Adam and Eve?

   _____

   _____

   _____

2. How did Satan cause Adam and Eve to doubt God's one command to them?

   _____

   _____

   _____

3. What were the consequences of Adam and Eve's sin?

   _____

   _____

   _____

4. Why did God decide to send the flood against the earth?

   _____

   _____

   _____

5. What agreement did God make with Noah?

   _____

   _____

   _____

UNDERSTAND THE STORY

Humanity's tragic rebellion against God in the garden impacted *everything*. The disobedience of Adam and Eve, and the rebellion of the generations that followed, took a God-ordained source of blessing and twisted it into a form of heartache. The stunning beauty and heart-wrenching tragedy of our world is explained and understood through these stories, helping us understand why something created so good has gone so terribly wrong.

God's Word shows us that human disobedience has universal implications. The choices and decisions that we make illustrate how we embrace or reject our Creator God. Although we tend to think of our choices as individual decisions that don't impact other people, this section of Genesis reveals that even a simple act—such as eating a forbidden fruit—can lead to suffering and death *for everyone*. The choices and decisions we make in this life are writing a moral drama, and our every deed illustrates how we embrace or reject our Creator.

The goodness of God's creation was not wholly destroyed by humanity's sin and rebellion. However, until the story is over, we cannot experience the good life that God intended for us apart from the taint of sin and the curse. As Paul wrote, "We know that the whole creation has been groaning as in the pains of childbirth" (Romans 8:22). We live in a fallen world today that is waiting to be redeemed and made new by the Creator.

1. What do the stories you have read this week reveal about the impact of sin?

   _____

   _____

   _____

   _____

2. How will these stories you have read help you to better shape your choices?

_____

_____

_____

_____

_____

LIVE THE STORY

Adam and Eve's expulsion from the garden was more than just a fair punishment for their disobedience. It was a continuation of God's perfect plan to be able to live in communion with the people whom he created. The garden would remain pure, and God would adjust his plan to give you and me the possibility of living there with him forever. Today, he is as passionate as ever in meeting us outside the garden and walking with us through every experience in life.

As we see from the story of Cain and Abel, the sin nature first birthed in Adam and Eve has been transmitted to their offspring. In fact, as the population on earth grew, it became clear that when given a choice, men and women chose evil over good. According to the Bible, God saw that mankind had become so wicked that "every inclination of the thoughts of the human heart was only evil all the time" (Genesis 6:5). Theologians call this the "doctrine of depravity." We are unable to "be good" on our own, leaving us unfit for God's community.

You would think this would be the end of the story—that God would have given up on us. But he didn't. This is perhaps the most mind-boggling thought in all the pages of Scripture: *in spite of our state of blatant selfishness and rebellion, God wanted us back.* Regardless of what Adam, Eve, Cain, and the descendants that followed did—and regardless of anything that *we* have done—God still wants to be with us. His upper story has not changed. He still wants to do life with us in a perfect and loving community of unified fellowship.

1. How will you be more intentional this week in pursuing a relationship with God?

_____

_____

_____

_____

_____

_____

2. What is one action you will take this week to put what you've learned into practice?

_____

_____

_____

_____

_____

_____

TELL THE STORY

The goal of this study is not only for you to understand the story of the Bible but also for you to share it with others. So, one day this week around a meal or your dinner table, have an intentional conversation about the topic of this session with family or friends. During your time together, read Genesis 1:1–31, and then use the following question for discussion:

Of all the things that God created, which is the one you find most interesting? Why?

Ask God this week to help you fully embrace the story of creation. Also, spend a few minutes each day committing the key verse to memory: "So God created mankind in his own image, in the image of God he created them; male and female he created them" (Genesis 1:27).

GOD BUILDS A NATION

GENESIS 12–36

WELCOME

Maybe you have heard the term *nation building* used in media news reports. The term generally refers to efforts in underdeveloped countries to rebuild after the ravages of war and corrupt leadership. Among other things, the process involves forming a government, establishing an economic system, creating an infrastructure of basic services (such as water and sanitation), setting up a legal and justice system, and providing protection from outsiders. Needless to say, it is a daunting endeavor, where new challenges and unexpected problems spring up daily. In this session, we will see that the way God chose to build his nation involved some of these same kinds of struggles. In fact, just to put his divine fingerprints on the process from day one, God chose to do it in ways that we would consider impossible.

VIDEO TEACHING NOTES

Welcome to session two of *God the Creator*. If there are any new members, take a moment to introduce yourselves to each other. Spend a few minutes sharing any insights or questions about last week's personal study. Then watch the video (see the streaming video access provided on the inside front cover) and use the following outline to record some of the main points. The answer key is found at the end of the session.

- The _____ story is how we see things from our perspective and the _____ story is how God sees things from his perspective.

- God begins to unveil his plan to get us back. He is going to create a brand-new _____. Through this _____, set apart for his purposes, he will reveal his _____, his power, and his plan to get us back.

- Why does God pick Abram and Sarai? He chooses them so that when people see this great _____, they will not see the _____ of Abram and Sarai, but their _____. They will see God as the one above the scenes of our lives.

- Abram's name, which ironically means "_____" in Hebrew, is changed to Abraham, which means "father of _____." Sarai's name, which means "_____" in Hebrew, is changed to Sarah, which means "_____."

- You think you have missed your chance to do something big and _____? That's the way we think in the lower story. But if we _____ our lives to God and what he's up to, some of our best years are still ahead of us.

- All the _____ and all the stories are woven together artistically by God to tell one very important _____ that promises to change our lives . . . forever.

GETTING STARTED

Begin your discussion by reciting the key verse and key idea together as a group. Now try to state the key verse from memory. On your first attempt, use your notes if you need help. On your second attempt, try to state it completely from memory.

KEY VERSE: "I will establish my covenant as an everlasting covenant between me and you and your descendants after you for the generations to come, to be your God and the God of your descendants after you" (Genesis 17:7).

KEY IDEA: God's first step in providing the way back into a relationship with him is to build a new nation. God establishes this nation on the most unqualified couple—Abraham and Sarah—who are old and childless. God chooses this pattern to show that he is behind the writing of this grand story of redemption.

GROUP DISCUSSION

Take a few minutes with your group members to discuss what you just watched and explore these concepts in Scripture.

1. What part of this week's teaching encouraged or challenged you the most? Why?

   _____

   _____

   _____

   _____

   _____

2. Why did God choose Abraham and Sarah to build his nation?

   _____

   _____

   _____

   _____

   _____

3. How can you relate to Sarah's desire to "help God" when his timing didn't match hers?

   _____

   _____

   _____

   _____

4. What do you find most unsettling in the story of God asking Abraham to sacrifice Isaac?

_____

_____

_____

_____

_____

5. What does the story of Abraham and Sarah tell you about the kinds of people God uses to fulfill his plans?

_____

_____

_____

_____

_____

6. What is your biggest takeaway as you reflect on what you learned this week?

_____

_____

_____

_____

CLOSING PRAYER

End your group time by sharing prayer requests, reviewing how God has answered past prayers, and praying for one another. Use the space below to record any requests and praises.

Also, make sure to pray for people God might add to your group—especially your neighbors.

Name   Request/Praise

_____   _____

_____   _____

_____   _____

_____   _____

_____   _____

_____   _____

_____   _____

FOR NEXT WEEK

Next week, we will look at the incredible highs and lows of Joseph's lower story journey from slavery to second in command over all of Egypt. Before your next group meeting, be sure to read through the following personal study, complete the exercises, and memorize the key verse for the session.

VIDEO NOTES ANSWER KEY

lower, upper / nation, nation, presence / nation, strength, weakness / father, many, princess, queen / significant, align / characters, story

PERSONAL STUDY

Take some time after your group meeting this week to read through this section and complete the personal study. In total, it should take about one hour to complete. Allow the Scripture to take root in your heart as you review the story of Abraham and the birth of the Hebrew nation.

KNOW THE STORY

There is a noticeable pattern in the Bible regarding the kind of people that God chooses to involve in his upper story. Generally, they are the kind of people who either feel that they are the least qualified person for the job, or that others feel are "disqualified" in some way. In this section of God's story, we find him choosing Abraham and Sarah to move humanity closer to fulfilling his plan for redemption. Both of them seem to be unlikely choices for the task.

> The LORD had said to Abram, "Go from your country, your people and your father's household to the land I will show you.
>
> "I will make you into a great nation,
>   and I will bless you;

I will make your name great,
     and you will be a blessing.
I will bless those who bless you,
     and whoever curses you I will curse;
and all peoples on earth
will be blessed through you."

So Abram went, as the LORD had told him; and Lot went with him. Abram was seventy-five years old when he set out from Harran. He took his wife Sarai, his nephew Lot, all the possessions they had accumulated and the people they had acquired in Harran, and they set out for the land of Canaan, and they arrived there (Genesis 12:1–5).

Now Sarai, Abram's wife, had borne him no children. But she had an Egyptian slave named Hagar; so she said to Abram, "The Lord has kept me from having children. Go, sleep with my slave; perhaps I can build a family through her."

Abram agreed to what Sarai said. So after Abram had been living in Canaan ten years, Sarai his wife took her Egyptian slave Hagar and gave her to her husband to be his wife. He slept with Hagar, and she conceived.

When she knew she was pregnant, she began to despise her mistress. Then Sarai said to Abram, "You are responsible for the wrong I am suffering. I put my slave in your arms, and now that she knows she is pregnant, she despises me. May the LORD judge between you and me."

"Your slave is in your hands," Abram said. "Do with her whatever you think best." Then Sarai mistreated Hagar; so she fled from her (Genesis 16:1–6).

When Abram was ninety-nine years old, the LORD appeared to him and said, "I am God Almighty; walk before me faithfully and be blameless. Then I will make my covenant between me and you and will greatly increase your numbers."

Abram fell facedown, and God said to him, "As for me, this is my covenant with you: You will be the father of many nations. No longer will you be called Abram; your name will be Abraham, for I have made you a father of many nations. I will make you very fruitful; I will make nations of you, and kings will come from you. I will establish my covenant as an everlasting covenant between me and you and your descendants after you for the generations to come, to be your God and the God of your descendants after you. The whole land of Canaan, where you now reside as a foreigner, I will give as an everlasting possession to you and your descendants after you; and I will be their God."...

God also said to Abraham, "As for Sarai your wife, you are no longer to call her Sarai; her name will be Sarah. I will bless her and will surely give you a son by her. I will bless her so that she will be the mother of nations; kings of peoples will come from her."

Abraham fell facedown; he laughed and said to himself, "Will a son be born to a man a hundred years old? Will Sarah bear a child at the age of ninety?" And Abraham said to God, "If only Ishmael might live under your blessing!" (Genesis 17:1–8, 15–18).

Now the LORD was gracious to Sarah as he had said, and the LORD did for Sarah what he had promised. Sarah became pregnant and bore a son to Abraham in his old age, at the very time God had promised him. Abraham gave the name

Isaac to the son Sarah bore him. When his son Isaac was eight days old, Abraham circumcised him, as God commanded him. Abraham was a hundred years old when his son Isaac was born to him.

Sarah said, "God has brought me laughter, and everyone who hears about this will laugh with me." And she added, "Who would have said to Abraham that Sarah would nurse children? Yet I have borne him a son in his old age."

The child grew and was weaned, and on the day Isaac was weaned Abraham held a great feast. But Sarah saw that the son whom Hagar the Egyptian had borne to Abraham was mocking, and she said to Abraham, "Get rid of that slave woman and her son, for that woman's son will never share in the inheritance with my son Isaac."

The matter distressed Abraham greatly because it concerned his son. But God said to him, "Do not be so distressed about the boy and your slave woman. Listen to whatever Sarah tells you, because it is through Isaac that your offspring will be reckoned. I will make the son of the slave into a nation also, because he is your offspring" (Genesis 21:1–13).

Some time later God tested Abraham. He said to him, "Abraham!"

"Here I am," he replied.

Then God said, "Take your son, your only son, whom you love—Isaac—and go to the region of Moriah. Sacrifice him there as a burnt offering on a mountain I will show you."

Early the next morning Abraham got up and loaded his donkey. He took with him two of his servants and his son Isaac. When he had cut enough wood for the burnt offering, he set out for the place God had told him about. On the third day Abraham looked up and saw the place in the distance. He said to his servants, "Stay here with the donkey while I and the boy go over there. We will worship and then we will come back to you."

Abraham took the wood for the burnt offering and placed it on his son Isaac, and he himself carried the fire and the knife. As the two of them went on together, Isaac spoke up and said to his father Abraham, "Father?"

"Yes, my son?" Abraham replied.

"The fire and wood are here," Isaac said, "but where is the lamb for the burnt offering?"

Abraham answered, "God himself will provide the lamb for the burnt offering, my son." And the two of them went on together.

When they reached the place God had told him about, Abraham built an altar there and arranged the wood on it. He bound his son Isaac and laid him on the altar, on top of the wood. Then he reached out his hand and took the knife to slay his son. But the angel of the LORD called out to him from heaven, "Abraham! Abraham!"

"Here I am," he replied.

"Do not lay a hand on the boy," he said. "Do not do anything to him. Now I know that you fear God, because you have not withheld from me your son, your only son."

Abraham looked up and there in a thicket he saw a ram caught by its horns. He went over and took the ram and sacrificed it as a burnt offering instead of his son. So Abraham called that place The LORD Will Provide. And to this day it is said, "On the mountain of the LORD it will be provided" (Genesis 22:1–14).

1. What promise did God make to Abraham at the start of his story? What was required of Abraham at that time so that promise could begin to be fulfilled?

_____

_____

_____

_____

2. What was Sarah's plan to secure an heir for Abraham when it appeared that God's plan was not going to happen? How did this work out for the couple in the end?

_____

_____

_____

_____

3. What was the significance of God changing the couple's names to Abraham ("father of many") and Sarah ("queen of a nation")?

_____

_____

_____

_____

4. How did Sarah respond when Isaac was finally born?

_____

_____

_____

_____

5. What was the ultimate purpose in God asking Abraham to sacrifice Isaac?

_____

_____

_____

_____

UNDERSTAND THE STORY

One of the first things we notice about the unfolding story of Scripture is that God does not need us to accomplish his purposes. In fact, he often accomplishes his plans in the most difficult way possible just to remind us that he is the one in charge. The story of Abraham is a perfect case in point. God determined to build a great nation in order to reveal himself to the world and ultimately bring about his plan of redemption. So who does he choose to found this great nation? None other than a man and woman well past the normal childbearing age.

It took great faith for Abraham and Sarah to trust in God's promises as the years passed. At times, this was an imperfect faith. Abraham lied to the Egyptians and told them Sarah was his sister. The couple tried to rush God's plans by securing an heir through Hagar. Both Abraham and Sarah laughed at separate times and doubted God's word that they would really have a son. Their faith was something like a roller coaster, down one second and up the next. Yet the Lord still chose to work through them to accomplish his plans.

It's hard to fault Abraham and Sarah for doubting and improvising at times. Twenty-five years is a long time to wait for a promise to be fulfilled. Believing you will start a family in your tenth decade of life isn't exactly buying into the conventional wisdom of the world. It is only to be expected that their faith would falter at times. But in the end, they chose to trust God and believe that what he said would come true—no matter how crazy it seemed. Abraham and Sarah passed the only test God cares about—the same one he puts in front of us today.

They trusted him. And because they did, the story continues.

1. What do the stories you have read this week reveal about the importance of faith?

   _____

   _____

   _____

   _____

2. How will these stories help you to trust God in spite of the circumstances?

   _____

   _____

   _____

   _____

LIVE THE STORY

Two thousand years after Abraham walked the earth, one of his descendants wrote a letter reminding the first followers of Jesus that "faith by itself, if it is not accompanied by action, is dead" (James 2:17). As James penned these words, he was no doubt thinking of his ancestor Abraham. Abraham's faith could certainly waver at times, yet he nevertheless had a persistent confidence that God would never break his promise. This trust was put to the test when God asked Abraham to sacrifice Isaac. Abraham was willing to *actively* put his trust in God by travelling to Mount Moriah and placing Isaac on the altar. Abraham knew that regardless of what God was asking him to do, he would be faithful to keep his promises. And so he obeyed God in faith. His story reveals that we must do the same in our lives—regardless of the cost.

1. What does *actively* trusting God look like in your life today?

   _____

   _____

   _____

2. What is one action you will take this week to put what you've learned into practice?

   _____

   _____

   _____

TELL THE STORY

One day this week around a meal or your dinner table, have an intentional conversation about the topic of this session with family or friends. During your time together, read

Genesis 12:1-9, and then use the following question for discussion:

What would it be like to leave everything behind like Abraham and move to a country that was completely foreign to you?

Ask God this week to help you fully embrace the story of Abraham. Also, spend a few minutes each day committing the key verse to memory: "I will establish my covenant as an everlasting covenant between me and you and your descendants after you for the generations to come, to be your God and the God of your descendants after you" (Genesis 17:7).

Session 3

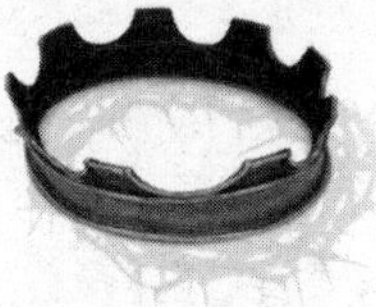

FROM SLAVE TO DEPUTY PHAROAH

GENESIS 37–50

WELCOME

Personal betrayal cuts us to the core. We decide to put our trust in someone—and that person we thought was on our side turns on us. It's bad enough when this happens between acquaintances, friends, or colleagues at work. But when a family member betrays, it's hard to keep going. The person that we will examine in this week's session knew the pain of family betrayal all too well. He came from the line that God had established through Abraham to build up a nation for himself. But this family certainly didn't function like any divine dynasty. They could barely get along with each other. We're not talking here about the normal rivalry that happens among family members—this person's brothers actually *left him to die.* The situation often looked bleak for him in the lower story. But in the upper story, God was using everything that he was going through for something much greater than he could have imagined.

— VIDEO TEACHING NOTES —

Welcome to session three of *God the Creator*. Spend a few minutes sharing any insights or questions about last week's personal study. Then watch the video (see the streaming video access provided on the inside front cover). The answer key is found at the end of the session.

- Joseph is a part of the nation that God in the upper story is slowly _____ to reveal his presence, his power, and his _____ to get all people back.

- In the lower story, the situation looks _____ for Joseph. But in the upper story, God has something quite _____ for him in mind.

- In the midst of Joseph's _____, a surprising sentence appears in the story: "The LORD was with Joseph so that he prospered" (Genesis 39:2). Even though God allowed Joseph's brothers to abuse him, God was now _____ him.

- When Joseph's brothers arrive in Egypt, they _____ before the second in command. Joseph is now thirty-nine years old. _____-_____

years have passed since he was sold down the river and thrown under the bus by his brothers.

- What Joseph's brothers did to him in the lower story was wrong and had lifelong _____. They really never could forgive themselves. But God used their sin-filled jealousy to _____ his overall purpose.

- Joseph's twenty-two years of up-and-down struggles _____ him into the kind of man who could do what he did with _____.

- The promise of God is that if we _____ him and align our lives to his upper story purposes, everything in our lives—the ups and downs, highs and hurts, praises and rejections—are all working together to accomplish _____.

GETTING STARTED

Begin your discussion by reciting the key verses and key idea together as a group. Now try to state the key verses from memory. On your first attempt, use your notes if you need help. On your second attempt, try to state it completely from memory.

Key Verses: "Don't be afraid. Am I in the place of God? You intended to harm me, but God intended it for good to accomplish what is now being done, the saving of many lives" (Genesis 50:19–20).

KEY IDEA: The nation of Israel is growing, but a devastating famine ahead threatens to wipe it out. So God intervenes by using the dysfunction of Joseph's family to save the nation. God orchestrates the affairs of Joseph so that he becomes second-in-command of all Egypt, where he can prepare for the famine. Through this dramatic event, the people of God are saved from extinction.

GROUP DISCUSSION

Take a few minutes with your group members to discuss what you just watched and explore these concepts in Scripture.

1. What part of this week's teaching encouraged or challenged you the most? Why?

2. In what ways can you relate to the jealousy and betrayal that Joseph experienced?

3. When have you seen God prosper you in the midst of trying circumstances?

4. How do you respond to the fact that God allowed Joseph to go through all of the trials and tragedies that he faced in order to fulfill the Lord's greater salvation plan?

5. What hope does the story of Joseph provide as you reflect on the painful situations that you have endured (or are currently enduring) in your life?

6. What is your biggest takeaway as you reflect on what you learned this week?

CLOSING PRAYER

End your group time by sharing prayer requests, reviewing how God has answered past prayers, and praying for one another. Use the space below to record any requests and praises. Also, make sure to pray for people God might add to your group—especially your neighbors.

Name   Request/Praise

_____   _____
_____   _____
_____   _____
_____   _____
_____   _____
_____   _____

FOR NEXT WEEK

Next week, we will look at the story of how God miraculously delivered the Israelites out of bondage in Egypt. Before your next group meeting, be sure to read through the following personal study, complete the exercises, and memorize the key verses for the session.

VIDEO NOTES ANSWER KEY

building, plan / bad, magnificent / trials, prospering /
bow, Twenty-two / consequences, accomplish / molded,
integrity / love, good

PERSONAL STUDY

Take some time after your group meeting this week to read through this section and complete the personal study. In total, it should take about one hour to complete. Allow the Scripture to take root in your heart and ask God to give you greater insights into Joseph's story.

KNOW THE STORY

We are introduced to Joseph when he was around seventeen years old. He is the son of Jacob, the grandson of Isaac, and the great-grandson of Abraham. Joseph became instrumental in God's upper story in two significant ways. First, he was directly responsible for saving the people of this budding nation of Israel from a terrible famine that threatened to extinguish them before they got started. Second, his story reveals God's incredible ability to transform the worst betrayals into sparkling examples of his own goodness, grace, forgiveness, and mercy.

> *Jacob lived in the land where his father had stayed, the land of Canaan.*
> *This is the account of Jacob's family line.*
> *Joseph, a young man of seventeen, was tending the flocks with his brothers, the sons of Bilhah and the sons of*

Zilpah, his father's wives, and he brought their father a bad report about them.

Now Israel loved Joseph more than any of his other sons, because he had been born to him in his old age; and he made an ornate robe for him. When his brothers saw that their father loved him more than any of them, they hated him and could not speak a kind word to him.

Joseph had a dream, and when he told it to his brothers, they hated him all the more. He said to them, "Listen to this dream I had: We were binding sheaves of grain out in the field when suddenly my sheaf rose and stood upright, while your sheaves gathered around mine and bowed down to it."

His brothers said to him, "Do you intend to reign over us? Will you actually rule us?" And they hated him all the more because of his dream and what he had said.

Then he had another dream, and he told it to his brothers. "Listen," he said, "I had another dream, and this time the sun and moon and eleven stars were bowing down to me."

When he told his father as well as his brothers, his father rebuked him and said, "What is this dream you had? Will your mother and I and your brothers actually come and bow down to the ground before you?" His brothers were jealous of him, but his father kept the matter in mind (Genesis 37:1–11).

So Joseph went after his brothers and found them near Dothan. But they saw him in the distance, and before he reached them, they plotted to kill him.

"Here comes that dreamer!" they said to each other. "Come now, let's kill him and throw him into one of these cisterns and say that a ferocious animal devoured him. Then we'll see what comes of his dreams."

When Reuben heard this, he tried to rescue him from their hands. "Let's not take his life," he said. "Don't shed any blood. Throw him into this cistern here in the wilderness, but don't lay a hand on him." Reuben said this to rescue him from them and take him back to his father.

So when Joseph came to his brothers, they stripped him of his robe—the ornate robe he was wearing—and they took him and threw him into the cistern. The cistern was empty; there was no water in it.

As they sat down to eat their meal, they looked up and saw a caravan of Ishmaelites coming from Gilead. Their camels were loaded with spices, balm and myrrh, and they were on their way to take them down to Egypt.

Judah said to his brothers, "What will we gain if we kill our brother and cover up his blood? Come, let's sell him to the Ishmaelites and not lay our hands on him; after all, he is our brother, our own flesh and blood." His brothers agreed.

So when the Midianite merchants came by, his brothers pulled Joseph up out of the cistern and sold him for twenty shekels of silver to the Ishmaelites, who took him to Egypt (Genesis 37:17–28).

Now Joseph had been taken down to Egypt. Potiphar, an Egyptian who was one of Pharaoh's officials, the captain of the guard, bought him from the Ishmaelites who had taken him there. The LORD was with Joseph so that he prospered, and he lived in the house of his Egyptian master. . . .

Now Joseph was well-built and handsome, and after a while his master's wife took notice of Joseph and said, "Come to bed with me!"

But he refused. "With me in charge," he told her, "my master does not concern himself with anything in the house; everything he owns he has entrusted to my care. No one is greater in this house than I am. My master has withheld nothing from me except you, because you are his wife. How then could I do such a wicked thing and sin against God?" And though she spoke to Joseph day after day, he refused to go to bed with her or even be with her.

One day he went into the house to attend to his duties, and none of the household servants was inside. She caught him by his cloak and said, "Come to bed with me!" But he left his cloak in her hand and ran out of the house.

When she saw that he had left his cloak in her hand and had run out of the house, she called her household servants. "Look," she said to them, "this Hebrew has been brought to us to make sport of us! He came in here to sleep with me, but I screamed. When he heard me scream for help, he left his cloak beside me and ran out of the house."

She kept his cloak beside her until his master came home. Then she told him this story: "That Hebrew slave you brought us came to me to make sport of me. But as soon as I screamed for help, he left his cloak beside me and ran out of the house."

When his master heard the story his wife told him, saying, "This is how your slave treated me," he burned with anger. Joseph's master took him and put him in prison, the place where the king's prisoners were confined (Genesis 39:1–2, 6–20).

So Pharaoh sent for Joseph, and he was quickly brought from the dungeon. When he had shaved and changed his clothes, he came before Pharaoh.

Pharaoh said to Joseph, "I had a dream, and no one can interpret it. But I have heard it said of you that when you hear a dream you can interpret it." . . .

Then Joseph said to Pharaoh, "The dreams of Pharaoh are one and the same. God has revealed to Pharaoh what he is about to do. The seven good cows are seven years, and the seven good heads of grain are seven years; it is one and the same dream. The seven lean, ugly cows that came up afterward are seven years, and so are the seven worthless heads of grain scorched by the east wind: They are seven years of famine.

"It is just as I said to Pharaoh: God has shown Pharaoh what he is about to do. Seven years of great abundance are coming throughout the land of Egypt, but seven years of famine will follow them. Then all the abundance in Egypt will be forgotten, and the famine will ravage the land. The abundance in the land will not be remembered, because the famine that follows it will be so severe. The reason the dream was given to Pharaoh in two forms is that the matter has been firmly decided by God, and God will do it soon.

"And now let Pharaoh look for a discerning and wise man and put him in charge of the land of Egypt. Let Pharaoh appoint commissioners over the land to take a fifth of the harvest of Egypt during the seven years of abundance. They should collect all the food of these good years that are coming and store up the grain under the authority of Pharaoh, to be kept in the cities for food. This food should be held in reserve for the country, to be used during the seven years of famine that will come upon Egypt, so that the country may not be ruined by the famine."

The plan seemed good to Pharaoh and to all his officials. So Pharaoh asked them, "Can we find anyone like this man, one in whom is the spirit of God?"

Then Pharaoh said to Joseph, "Since God has made all this known to you, there is no one so discerning and wise as you. You shall be in charge of my palace, and all my people are to submit to your orders. Only with respect to the throne will I be greater than you." (Genesis 41:14–15, 25–40).

When Jacob learned that there was grain in Egypt, he said to his sons, "Why do you just keep looking at each other?" He continued, "I have heard that there is grain in Egypt. Go down there and buy some for us, so that we may live and not die."

Then ten of Joseph's brothers went down to buy grain from Egypt. But Jacob did not send Benjamin, Joseph's brother, with the others, because he was afraid that harm might come to him. So Israel's sons were among those who went to buy grain, for there was famine in the land of Canaan also.

Now Joseph was the governor of the land, the person who sold grain to all its people. So when Joseph's brothers arrived, they bowed down to him with their faces to the ground. As soon as Joseph saw his brothers, he recognized them, but he pretended to be a stranger and spoke harshly to them. "Where do you come from?" he asked (Genesis 42:1–7).

Then Joseph could no longer control himself before all his attendants, and he cried out, "Have everyone leave my presence!" So there was no one with Joseph when he made himself known to his brothers. And he wept so loudly that the Egyptians heard him, and Pharaoh's household heard about it.

Joseph said to his brothers, "I am Joseph! Is my father still living?" But his brothers were not able to answer him, because they were terrified at his presence.

Then Joseph said to his brothers, "Come close to me." When they had done so, he said, "I am your brother Joseph, the one you sold into Egypt! And now, do not be distressed and do not be angry with yourselves for selling me here, because it was to save lives that God sent me ahead of you. For two years now there has been famine in the land, and for the next five years there will be no plowing and reaping. But God sent me ahead of you to preserve for you a remnant on earth and to save your lives by a great deliverance.

"So then, it was not you who sent me here, but God. He made me father to Pharaoh, lord of his entire household and ruler of all Egypt (Genesis 45:1–8).

When Joseph's brothers saw that their father was dead, they said, "What if Joseph holds a grudge against us and pays us back for all the wrongs we did to him?" So they sent word to Joseph, saying, "Your father left these instructions before he died: 'This is what you are to say to Joseph: I ask you to forgive your brothers the sins and the wrongs they committed in treating you so badly.' Now please forgive the sins of the servants of the God of your father." When their message came to him, Joseph wept.

His brothers then came and threw themselves down before him. "We are your slaves," they said.

But Joseph said to them, "Don't be afraid. Am I in the place of God? You intended to harm me, but God intended it for good to accomplish what is now being done, the saving of many lives. So then, don't be afraid. I will provide for you and your children" (Genesis 50:15–21).

1. What caused Joseph's brothers to despise him?

2. How did Joseph respond to the advances of Potiphar's wife?

3. What warning and advice did Joseph give in interpreting Pharaoh's dreams?

4. What events brought about the reuniting of Joseph and his brothers?

5. What did Joseph say to his brothers to reassure them he
   was not holding a grudge?

   _____

   _____

   _____

   _____

   _____

——— UNDERSTAND THE STORY ———

One of the central themes of the Old Testament is that God always keeps his promises to his people. Whether extending his hand of blessing or the rod of judgment, at every point God works to fulfill his covenant promises to Abraham. In the life of Joseph, we see the great lengths to which God will go to preserve his chosen people and bring his promises to fulfillment.

Little did Joseph's brothers realize when they sold him into slavery that God would turn their act of jealous hatred into a method of salvation for his people. They had intended only evil toward their brother, but in the end, their rebellious and selfish actions only became part of God's greater redemption story. God's good purpose *always* triumphs.

For the brothers, coming face-to-face with the one whom they had betrayed was an earth-shaking encounter. Joseph was no longer the little brother they could push around. He was a powerful ruler who could have thrown them into a dark place or consigned them to lives of slavery. But Joseph did not harbor a desire for vengeance, for he understood that everything in his life had been orchestrated by God. Joseph's belief that God was in charge freed him to forgive his brothers. He understood God's greater plan for the family of Abraham.

1. What do the stories you have read this week reveal about God's ability to turn even the worst situations into something good?

   _____

   _____

   _____

   _____

   _____

2. How will these stories help you to see your trials in a new light?

   _____

   _____

   _____

   _____

   _____

LIVE THE STORY

How did Joseph have such an amazing attitude through all his ordeals? How was he able to forgive his brothers after everything they had done to him? Somewhere along the journey, he had caught a glimpse of God's upper story plan. When we likewise align our lives to God's upper story, it enables us to reframe everything we experience in our lower story. We come to believe that whatever we encounter in this life—the ups and downs, the mountaintops and the valleys, the good and bad—are all working together to accomplish good. We begin to truly believe in our hearts, as Paul would later write, that "in all things God works for the good of those who love him, who have been called according to his purpose" (Romans 8:28). As we do this and live out our lower story, we step into the role that God has for us in his upper story.

1. How has God used certain events in your life to shape you into who you are today?

2. What is one action you will take this week to put what you've learned into practice?

TELL THE STORY

One day around a meal or your dinner table, have an intentional conversation about this week's topic with family or friends. During your time together, read Genesis 45:1–11, and then use the following question for discussion:

How can things that first appear to be negative turn out to be positive?

Ask God this week to help you fully embrace the story of Joseph and his brothers. Also, spend a few minutes each day committing the key verses to memory: "Don't be afraid. Am I in the place of God? You intended to harm me, but God intended it for good to accomplish what is now being done, the saving of many lives" (Genesis 50:19–20).

DELIVERANCE

EXODUS 1–17

WELCOME

From a lower story perspective, it seemed that God's plan to create a new nation had faltered. The Lord had brought his people, the Israelites, into the land of Egypt to escape a famine. They had flourished there and grown in numbers. But the size of their population had now caused the leadership of Egypt to fear they might take over the land. As a result, the king of Egypt (known as the "pharaoh") began to enslave the Israelites. He placed cruel slave masters over them who forced them to work from sunup until sundown, building such massive structures as the now-famous pyramids. But as we will discover in this session, these events did not take God by surprise. He was getting ready to unveil his greater plan of restoration. And, true to form, this plan would involve one of the most unlikely of characters.

— VIDEO TEACHING NOTES —

Welcome to session four of *God the Creator*. Spend a few minutes sharing any insights or questions about last week's personal study. Then watch the video (see the streaming video access provided on the inside front cover). The answer key is found at the end of the session.

- At the opening of today's story, something has gone terribly _____. The nation of Israel—the people whom God is going to use to bring us back into a relationship with himself—finds themselves in deep _____.

- The time has come for God to _____ Israel and restore them on the path toward his promise to them. It is time to once again reveal his _____, his power, and his plan. He just needs the right _____.

- _____ has a shaky past with Egypt. He has burned some bridges that would seem to make him a poor candidate to deliver God's _____.

- God sees it differently. In the upper story, he sees Moses' weakness as the best _____ for his strength. When Israel is successful in being freed from the Egyptian _____, everyone will see God.

- In Hebrew, "____" is pronounced Yahweh. This name for God implies that he is the self-existent One—the one who always was, always is, and always will be—the faithful and _____ God who calls himself "I AM."

- There is a major clue to God's plan within this event called the _____. The way in which we will be saved from eternal death will require the _____ of an unblemished Lamb be placed over the "doorpost" of our lives.

GETTING STARTED

Begin your discussion by reciting the key verse and key idea together as a group. Now try to state the key verse from memory. On your first attempt, use your notes if you need help. On your second attempt, try to state it completely from memory.

KEY VERSE: "Commemorate this day, the day you came out of Egypt, out of the land of slavery, because the LORD brought you out of it with a mighty hand" (Exodus 13:3).

KEY IDEA: God had placed the Israelites in the land of Egypt to grow, prosper, and maintain their purity as a nation. He had warned his people that for a period of time the Egyptians would enslave and mistreat them, but he would ultimately deliver them. All this came to pass just as God said. God used these events to reveal his upper-story plan to redeem all people through the Passover Lamb.

GROUP DISCUSSION

Take a few minutes with your group members to discuss what you just watched and explore these concepts in Scripture.

1. What part of this week's teaching encouraged or challenged you the most? Why?

2. Why did God choose Moses to lead the Israelites out of Egypt?

3. How can you relate to Moses' fear that he was not the best candidate for God's plans?

4. What do you find most unsettling about the plagues that God sent against Egypt?

5. What does the story of Moses tell you about the kind of leaders the Lord is seeking?

_____

_____

_____

_____

6. What is your biggest takeaway as you reflect on what you learned this week?

_____

_____

_____

_____

CLOSING PRAYER

End your group time by sharing prayer requests, reviewing how God has answered past prayers, and praying for one another. Use the space below to record any requests and praises. Also, make sure to pray for people God might add to your group—especially your neighbors.

Name   Request/Praise

_____   _____

_____   _____

_____   _____

_____   _____

_____   _____

FOR NEXT WEEK

Next week, we will look at how the Israelites' lack of trust in God to take the Promised Land resulted in serious consequences. Before your next group meeting, be sure to read through the following personal study, complete the exercises, and memorize the key verse for the session.

VIDEO NOTES ANSWER KEY

wrong, trouble / deliver, name, person / Moses, message / channel, oppression/ "I AM," dependable / Passover, blood

PERSONAL STUDY

Take some time after your group meeting this week to read through this section and complete the personal study. In total, it should take about one hour to complete. Allow the Scripture to take root in your heart as you review the story of the deliverance of the Israelites.

KNOW THE STORY

For nearly 400 years, the people of Israel had lived in relative freedom in Egypt. But as the events of Exodus unfold, it is clear that the Egyptians had changed their attitude toward the Israelites. While it is difficult to establish an exact historical timeline, it is likely that Egypt had just emerged from the leadership of a foreign people, the Hyksos, who had ruled Lower Egypt for more than 100 years. If this is correct, it could explain the antagonism the Egyptians held toward the Hebrews, who represented a rising foreign power within their own land.

> Now Joseph and all his brothers and all that generation died, but the Israelites were exceedingly fruitful; they multiplied greatly, increased in numbers and became so numerous that the land was filled with them.
>
> Then a new king, to whom Joseph meant nothing, came to power in Egypt. "Look," he said to his people, "the Israelites

have become far too numerous for us. Come, we must deal shrewdly with them or they will become even more numerous and, if war breaks out, will join our enemies, fight against us and leave the country."

So they put slave masters over them to oppress them with forced labor, and they built Pithom and Rameses as store cities for Pharaoh. But the more they were oppressed, the more they multiplied and spread; so the Egyptians came to dread the Israelites and worked them ruthlessly (Exodus 1:6–13).

One day, after Moses had grown up, he went out to where his own people were and watched them at their hard labor. He saw an Egyptian beating a Hebrew, one of his own people. Looking this way and that and seeing no one, he killed the Egyptian and hid him in the sand. The next day he went out and saw two Hebrews fighting. He asked the one in the wrong, "Why are you hitting your fellow Hebrew?"

The man said, "Who made you ruler and judge over us? Are you thinking of killing me as you killed the Egyptian?" Then Moses was afraid and thought, "What I did must have become known."

When Pharaoh heard of this, he tried to kill Moses, but Moses fled from Pharaoh and went to live in Midian, where he sat down by a well. Now a priest of Midian had seven daughters, and they came to draw water and fill the troughs to water their father's flock. Some shepherds came along and drove them away, but Moses got up and came to their rescue and watered their flock. . . .

During that long period, the king of Egypt died. The Israelites groaned in their slavery and cried out, and their cry for help because of their slavery went up to God. God heard their groaning and he remembered his covenant with Abraham, with Isaac and with Jacob. So God looked on the Israelites and was concerned about them (Exodus 2:11–17, 23–25).

Now Moses was tending the flock of Jethro his father-in-law, the priest of Midian, and he led the flock to the far side of the wilderness and came to Horeb, the mountain of God. There the angel of the LORD appeared to him in flames of fire from within a bush. Moses saw that though the bush was on fire it did not burn up. So Moses thought, "I will go over and see this strange sight—why the bush does not burn up."

When the LORD saw that he had gone over to look, God called to him from within the bush, "Moses! Moses!"

And Moses said, "Here I am."

"Do not come any closer," God said. "Take off your sandals, for the place where you are standing is holy ground." Then he said, "I am the God of your father, the God of Abraham, the God of Isaac and the God of Jacob." At this, Moses hid his face, because he was afraid to look at God.

The LORD said, "I have indeed seen the misery of my people in Egypt. I have heard them crying out because of their slave drivers, and I am concerned about their suffering. So I have come down to rescue them from the hand of the Egyptians and to bring them up out of that land into a good and spacious land, a land flowing with milk and honey. . . . "

Moses said to God, "Suppose I go to the Israelites and say to them, 'The God of your fathers has sent me to you,' and they ask me, 'What is his name?' Then what shall I tell them?"

God said to Moses, "I AM WHO I AM. This is what you are to say to the Israelites: 'I AM has sent me to you'" (Exodus 3:1–8, 13–14).

Then the LORD said to Moses, "See, I have made you like God to Pharaoh, and your brother Aaron will be your prophet. You are to say everything I command you, and your brother Aaron is to tell Pharaoh to let the Israelites go out of his country. But I will harden Pharaoh's heart, and though I multiply my signs and wonders in Egypt, he will not listen to you. Then I will lay my hand on Egypt and with mighty acts of judgment I will bring out my divisions, my people the Israelites. And the Egyptians will know that I am the LORD when I stretch out my hand against Egypt and bring the Israelites out of it."

Moses and Aaron did just as the LORD commanded them. Moses was eighty years old and Aaron eighty-three when they spoke to Pharaoh (Exodus 7:1–7).

Now the LORD had said to Moses, "I will bring one more plague on Pharaoh and on Egypt. After that, he will let you go from here, and when he does, he will drive you out completely. Tell the people that men and women alike are to ask their neighbors for articles of silver and gold." (The LORD made the Egyptians favorably disposed toward the people, and Moses himself was highly regarded in Egypt by Pharaoh's officials and by the people.)

So Moses said, "This is what the LORD says: 'About midnight I will go throughout Egypt. Every firstborn son in Egypt will die, from the firstborn son of Pharaoh, who sits on the throne, to the firstborn son of the female slave, who is at her hand mill, and all the firstborn of the cattle as well. There will be loud wailing throughout Egypt—worse than there has ever been or ever will be again. But among the Israelites not a dog will bark at any person or animal.' Then you will know that the LORD makes a distinction between Egypt and Israel. All these officials of yours will come to me, bowing down before me and saying, 'Go, you and all the people who follow you!' After that I will leave." Then Moses, hot with anger, left Pharaoh.

The LORD had said to Moses, "Pharaoh will refuse to listen to you—so that my wonders may be multiplied in Egypt." Moses and Aaron performed all these wonders before Pharaoh, but the LORD hardened Pharaoh's heart, and he would not let the Israelites go out of his country (Exodus 11:1–10).

During the night Pharaoh summoned Moses and Aaron and said, "Up! Leave my people, you and the Israelites! Go, worship the LORD as you have requested. Take your flocks and herds, as you have said, and go. And also bless me."

The Egyptians urged the people to hurry and leave the country. "For otherwise," they said, "we will all die!" So the people took their dough before the yeast was added, and carried it on their shoulders in kneading troughs wrapped in clothing. The Israelites did as Moses instructed and asked the Egyptians for articles of silver and gold and for clothing. The LORD had made the Egyptians favorably disposed toward the people, and they gave them what they asked for; so they plundered the Egyptians (Exodus 12:31–36).

1. What reason did Pharaoh give for oppressing the people of Israel?

2. What caused Moses to flee to the land of Midian?

3. What did God tell Moses that he had come to do?

4. What was to happen during the final plague?

5. What were the Israelites allowed to take with them as they left Egypt?

——— UNDERSTAND THE STORY ———

God reveals himself in the story of the Exodus as the mover of empires who has authority over the kings of the earth. The Israelites discovered through the ten plagues that their Lord was much more than a regional or tribal deity. His power could not be matched by any other god.

It is nearly impossible to overstate the faith-shaking effect the ten plagues must have had on the Egyptian people. Each plague put one of their deities in the cross-hairs and brought it down. Through these judgments, God was not only punishing Pharaoh for his disobedience, but he was also asserting his power and authority over all the Egyptian gods. He was destroying the very foundations of Egyptian power and rule!

The final plague brought about the death of every firstborn in Egypt. The Lord decreed the angel of death would only "pass over" those homes that had placed the blood of a lamb on their doorposts. This sacrifice, the Passover, lies at the heart of the Old Testament story and would be memorialized forever after by God's people in an annual celebration. The plague broke Pharaoh's hardened heart and led to the Israelites' redemption and deliverance in the lower story. But even more, it points to a greater story of redemption and deliverance in the upper story that was through the sacrifice of God's firstborn Son on a cross.

1. What do the stories you have read this week reveal about the way God responds to the cries of his people?

2. How will these stories help you to know that God understands your situations and hears your cries to him for help?

_____

_____

_____

—— LIVE THE STORY ——

Perhaps you can relate to the Israelites' situation. You have a "pharaoh" in your life—a harmful person, troubling circumstance, or conflicted situation—and it feels as if that personal pharaoh is in complete control. But the story of the Israelites' deliverance reveals that while it may *seem* this pharaoh is in control, God is *actually* in control and aware of your plight. He promises to you today what he promised to Moses: "I will be with you" (Exodus 3:12). He will do for you what he did for the Israelites. If you love him, align your life to his plan, and take the steps he directs, he will lead you through your own Red Sea. God will always provide a way through obstacles that may seem insurmountable. It may seem scary at times to follow his lead . . . but as you do, you will find that he is leading you to a place of health, wholeness, and restoration.

1. What are some areas in your life where you need to experience freedom today?

_____

_____

_____

2. What is one action you will take this week to put what you've learned into practice?

_____

_____

_____

_____

_____

TELL THE STORY

One day around a meal or your dinner table, have an intentional conversation about this week's topic with family or friends. During your time together, read Exodus 13:3–10, and then use the following question for discussion:

What are some examples of how God has provided for you in big ways?

Ask God this week to help you fully embrace the story of Israel's deliverance. Also, spend a few minutes each day committing the key verse to memory: "Commemorate this day, the day you came out of Egypt, out of the land of slavery, because the Lord brought you out of it with a mighty hand" (Exodus 13:3).

WANDERINGS

EXODUS 18–NUMBERS 27

WELCOME

There's nothing quite like taking a family road trip for vacation. It's such a great feeling to arrive at your destination and witness something spectacular that you haven't seen before. Of course, if your family was like most, the *process* of getting there was not as spectacular. When you're crammed into a tight space for hours, the people you are with—no matter how much you love them—can start to get on your nerves. The monotony breeds boredom and bickering. Even worse is when the driver takes a wrong turn. You can quickly end up in the wrong place and wandering around in circles. In this session, we will see that the Israelites encountered many of these same problems on their "road trip" to the Promised Land. The journey caused them to bicker, grumble, and complain against Moses. But even worse, a wrong turn would cause them a delay in reaching their destination—a serious delay to the tune of *forty years*.

VIDEO TEACHING NOTES

Welcome to session five of *God the Creator*. Spend a few minutes sharing any insights or questions about last week's personal study. Then watch the video (see the streaming video access provided on the inside front cover) The answer key is found at the end of the session.

- It is in our nature to "stand up on the inside." It is in our nature to struggle with _____ and other people telling us what to do. It's why many of us have a hard time with God and the _____ .

- In God's _____, people are treated with full dignity and respect—no hurting, no hurling, no hoarding, no attacks, no withdrawing. This is what the Ten Commandments seek to _____ in our lives.

- Three instances of the Israelites' fighting and complaining are recorded. First, they complain about their general _____ . Second, they complain about the _____ they have to eat. Third, they question why God only speaks to _____ .

- The Israelites decide not to move forward out of _____ . So God has them make a U-Turn back down south again, along the Red Sea, back deep into the wilderness. It will turn into a _____ detour.

- Our life is like a road trip. God wants to _____ us every step of the way. He sees the picture from the upper story and wants the best for us. He wants us to make it to the final _____. But we have to trust him.

- God has a place of _____ where he wants to take us. In that place, as we live for Him, we will also be a _____ to the other people around us.

GETTING STARTED

Begin your discussion by reciting the key verses and key idea together as a group. Now try to state the key verses from memory. On your first attempt, use your notes if you need help. On your second attempt, try to state it completely from memory.

Key Verses: "If the LORD is pleased with us, he will lead us into that land, a land flowing with milk and honey, and will give it to us. Only do not rebel against the LORD" (Numbers 14:8–9).

KEY IDEA: It's time for the Israelites to move into the Promised Land. In preparation, God gives them commandments on how to love him and their neighbors. Once the Israelites take the land, the surrounding nations will be able to see that God's redemption plan includes even them. But the Israelites are overwhelmed by the task and refuse to move ahead. So

God sends them back into the wilderness until the unbelieving generation dies. Once the forty years have passed, God will give the next generation another opportunity to enter.

GROUP DISCUSSION

Take a few minutes with your group members to discuss what you just watched and explore these concepts in Scripture.

1. What part of this week's teaching encouraged or challenged you the most? Why?

2. What was God's purpose in giving the Ten Commandments to his people?

3. How can you relate to the Israelites' fears when asked to take the Promised Land?

4. What do you find most unsettling about the consequences the Israelites received as a result of their lack of trust in God's promises?

_____

_____

_____

_____

5. When is a time that God challenged you to trust him when you were facing a challenging and overwhelming situation? What happened as a result?

_____

_____

_____

_____

6. What is your biggest takeaway as you reflect on what you learned this week?

_____

_____

_____

CLOSING PRAYER

End your group time by sharing prayer requests, reviewing how God has answered past prayers, and praying for one another. Use the space below to record any requests and praises.

Also, make sure to pray for people God might add to your group—especially your neighbors.

Name	Request/Praise

FOR NEXT WEEK

Next week, we will look at how God continues to unfold his upper-story plan through Joshua and the Israelites' conquest of the Promised Land. Before your next group meeting, be sure to read through the following personal study, complete the exercises, and memorize the key verses for the session.

VIDEO NOTES ANSWER KEY

authority, Ten Commandments / community,
accomplish / hardship, food, Moses / fear, forty-year / lead,
destination / blessing, blessing

PERSONAL STUDY

Take some time after your group meeting this week to read through this section and complete the personal study. In total, it should take about one hour to complete. Allow the Scripture to take root in your heart as you review the story of the wandering Israelites.

KNOW THE STORY

God's upper story started in a garden—a perfect environment where he could enjoy a relationship with his creation. But when Adam and Eve sinned, the Lord had to forever banish humanity from that garden. So God took another approach. He created a nation and determined to reveal himself to them. After preserving his people from famine, rescuing them from slavery, and giving them rules for living, he was ready to lead this people into another garden: Canaan. The only question was . . . would they choose to enter into it?

On the first day of the third month after the Israelites left Egypt—on that very day—they came to the Desert of Sinai. After they set out from Rephidim, they entered the Desert of Sinai, and Israel camped there in the desert in front of the mountain.

Then Moses went up to God, and the LORD called to him from the mountain and said, "This is what you are to say to the descendants of Jacob and what you are to tell the people of Israel: 'You yourselves have seen what I did to Egypt, and how I carried you on eagles' wings and brought you to myself. Now if you obey me fully and keep my covenant, then out of all nations you will be my treasured possession. Although the whole earth is mine, you will be for me a kingdom of priests and a holy nation.' These are the words you are to speak to the Israelites."

So Moses went back and summoned the elders of the people and set before them all the words the LORD had commanded him to speak. The people all responded together, "We will do everything the LORD has said." So Moses brought their answer back to the LORD.

The LORD said to Moses, "I am going to come to you in a dense cloud, so that the people will hear me speaking with you and will always put their trust in you." Then Moses told the LORD what the people had said. . . .

On the morning of the third day there was thunder and lightning, with a thick cloud over the mountain, and a very loud trumpet blast. Everyone in the camp trembled. Then Moses led the people out of the camp to meet with God, and they stood at the foot of the mountain (Exodus 19:1–9, 16–17).

And God spoke all these words:

"I am the LORD your God, who brought you out of Egypt, out of the land of slavery.

"You shall have no other gods before me.

"You shall not make for yourself an image in the form of anything in heaven above or on the earth beneath or in the waters below. You shall not bow down to them or worship them; for I, the LORD your God, am a jealous God,

punishing the children for the sin of the parents to the third and fourth generation of those who hate me, but showing love to a thousand generations of those who love me and keep my commandments.

"You shall not misuse the name of the LORD your God, for the LORD will not hold anyone guiltless who misuses his name.

"Remember the Sabbath day by keeping it holy. Six days you shall labor and do all your work, but the seventh day is a sabbath to the LORD your God. On it you shall not do any work, neither you, nor your son or daughter, nor your male or female servant, nor your animals, nor any foreigner residing in your towns. For in six days the LORD made the heavens and the earth, the sea, and all that is in them, but he rested on the seventh day. Therefore the LORD blessed the Sabbath day and made it holy.

"Honor your father and your mother, so that you may live long in the land the LORD your God is giving you.

"You shall not murder.

"You shall not commit adultery.

"You shall not steal.

"You shall not give false testimony against your neighbor.

"You shall not covet your neighbor's house. You shall not covet your neighbor's wife, or his male or female servant, his ox or donkey, or anything that belongs to your neighbor" (Exodus 20:1–17).

Now the people complained about their hardships in the hearing of the LORD, and when he heard them his anger was aroused. Then fire from the LORD burned among them and consumed some of the outskirts of the camp. When the people cried out to Moses, he prayed to the LORD and the fire died down. So that place was called Taberah, because fire from the LORD had burned among them.

The rabble with them began to crave other food, and again the Israelites started wailing and said, "If only we had meat to eat! We remember the fish we ate in Egypt at no cost—also the cucumbers, melons, leeks, onions and garlic. But now we have lost our appetite; we never see anything but this manna!" . . .

Now a wind went out from the LORD and drove quail in from the sea. It scattered them up to two cubits deep all around the camp, as far as a day's walk in any direction. All that day and night and all the next day the people went out and gathered quail. No one gathered less than ten homers. Then they spread them out all around the camp. But while the meat was still between their teeth and before it could be consumed, the anger of the LORD burned against the people, and he struck them with a severe plague. Therefore the place was named Kibroth Hattaavah, because there they buried the people who had craved other food (Numbers 11:1–6, 31–34).

The LORD said to Moses, "Send some men to explore the land of Canaan, which I am giving to the Israelites. From each ancestral tribe send one of its leaders."

So at the LORD's command Moses sent them out from the Desert of Paran. All of them were leaders of the Israelites. . . .

They came back to Moses and Aaron and the whole Israelite community at Kadesh in the Desert of Paran. There they reported to them and to the whole assembly and showed them the fruit of the land. They gave Moses this account: "We went into the land to which you sent us, and it does flow with milk and honey! Here is its fruit. But the people who live

*there are powerful, and the cities are fortified and very large.
We even saw descendants of Anak there. The Amalekites live
in the Negev; the Hittites, Jebusites and Amorites live in the
hill country; and the Canaanites live near the sea and along
the Jordan."*

*Then Caleb silenced the people before Moses and said,
"We should go up and take possession of the land, for we can
certainly do it."*

*But the men who had gone up with him said, "We can't
attack those people; they are stronger than we are." And
they spread among the Israelites a bad report about the land
they had explored. They said, "The land we explored de-
vours those living in it. All the people we saw there are of
great size. We saw the Nephilim there (the descendants of
Anak come from the Nephilim). We seemed like grasshop-
pers in our own eyes, and we looked the same to them"*
(Numbers 13:1–3, 26–33).

*The LORD replied, "I have forgiven them, as you asked. Nev-
ertheless, as surely as I live and as surely as the glory of the
LORD fills the whole earth, not one of those who saw my glory
and the signs I performed in Egypt and in the wilderness but
who disobeyed me and tested me ten times— not one of them
will ever see the land I promised on oath to their ancestors.
No one who has treated me with contempt will ever see it. But
because my servant Caleb has a different spirit and follows
me wholeheartedly, I will bring him into the land he went to,
and his descendants will inherit it. Since the Amalekites and
the Canaanites are living in the valleys, turn back tomorrow
and set out toward the desert along the route to the Red Sea"*
(Numbers 14:20–25).

1. How did God make his presence known to the people at Mount Sinai?

2. What were God's restrictions about the making of images or idols?

3. What were the results of the people's complaints against God?

4. What was the report of the men who had gone to explore that land of Canaan?

5. What were the consequences for the people of not entering into Canaan?

_____

_____

_____

_____

UNDERSTAND THE STORY

The greatest enemy of faith is forgetfulness. The Israelites camped at Mount Sinai for more than a year. Every day, they witnessed evidence of God's reality and power. They were saved from their idolatry. They built the tabernacle and saw God's presence fill it. After all this, one would think they would walk faithfully before the Lord. But sadly, that is not what happened.

Shortly after the Israelites departed from Sinai, they descended into constant grumbling. They complained about their general hardships. They complained about the manna they were given to eat. Moses' brother and sister even complained about his leadership and whether the Lord only spoke through him. Even worse, after finally reaching the Promised Land, the people complained the task was too great and refused to trust that God would lead them.

Of course, it is easy to criticize the Israelites and their desire to go back to Egypt. But how often do we look with longing at things that we know deep down have always led to heartache? We also forget just how faithful the Lord has been to us. Israel had seen God's awesome deliverance. They had seen him work wonders in Egypt. But when times grew rough, their forgetfulness led them to minimize both the horror of slavery and the goodness of God.

1. What do the stories you have read this week reveal about the importance of remembering God's faithfulness?

_____

_____

_____

_____

2. How will these stories help you to trust your future to God?

_____

_____

_____

_____

LIVE THE STORY

When we read the Israelites' story, it can be tempting to conclude that God is mean-spirited. So what if the people grumbled at times? So what if they had second thoughts about leaving Egypt? And shouldn't God cut them a little slack for being afraid of *giants*? As it turns out, from an upper story view, this *is* a big deal. God is building a special nation . . . and that nation can only succeed if the people place their complete trust in him. In the same way, it's a big deal for us to put our complete trust in God. He wants to lead us to incredible things in life, but we won't get there unless we put our complete faith in him. When he calls out "left," we need to go left. When he says "stop," we need to halt dead in our tracks. And when he implores, "Bust through the barrier, no matter how bad it looks," we need to charge ahead in faith.

1. What is an area in your life where you are still trying to assert control?

2. What is one action you will take this week to put what you've learned into practice?

TELL THE STORY

One day around a meal or your dinner table, have an intentional conversation about this week's topic with family or friends. During your time together, read Exodus 19:10–25, and then use the following question for discussion:

What are some of the ways that God dwells among us today?

Ask God this week to help you fully embrace the story of the wandering Israelites. Also, spend a few minutes each day committing the key verses to memory: "If the LORD is pleased with us, he will lead us into that land, a land flowing with milk and honey, and will give it to us. Only do not rebel against the LORD" (Numbers 14:8–9).

THE BATTLE BEGINS

JOSHUA 1–24

WELCOME

Forty years had passed, and the unbelieving generation of Israelites that had refused to enter the Promised Land had now died in the wilderness. Under the leadership of Joshua, the next generation of Israelites would have a fresh opportunity to trust God and succeed where the previous generation had failed. Back then, Joshua had been one of twelve spies whom Moses had selected to sneak into Canaan and report back. He had urged the people to trust God and take the land. But they would not listen. Now, with Moses dead, God told the courageous captain it was time to try again. Would they listen this time? Or would history repeat itself?

VIDEO TEACHING NOTES

Welcome to session six of *God the Creator*. Spend a few minutes sharing any insights or questions about last week's personal study. Then watch the video (see the streaming video access provided on the inside front cover) The answer key is found at the end of the session.

- The Israelites were faced with such an _____ challenge. It is time for them to enter the land that God promised to give to them _____ years earlier.

- In order for the people to be strong and courageous, they needed three things. First, they needed to be people of the _____. God told Joshua, "Keep this Book of the Law always on your lips; meditate on it " (Joshua 1:8).

- Second, they needed to be people of _____. God told Joshua that he could be strong and _____ because the Lord would be with him.

- Third, they needed to be people _____ with God. Before the Israelites engaged in their first battle, God instructed all the males to be circumcised. Circumcision outwardly identified them as _____ to God.

- We all face battles in our lives. Like Joshua and the children of Israel, we need to be people of the _____, people of _____, and people _____ with God. With God on our side, we will be _____.

- In the lower story, the _____ are bigger than we are. In the upper story, God is bigger than our _____ .

GETTING STARTED

Begin your discussion by reciting the key verse and key idea together as a group. Now try to state the key verse from memory. On your first attempt, use your notes if you need help. On your second attempt, try to state it completely from memory.

> **KEY VERSE:** "Be strong and courageous. Do not be afraid; do not be discouraged, for the Lord your God will be with you wherever you go" (Joshua 1:9).

> **KEY IDEA:** From an upper story perspective, God had been patient with the people of Canaan, giving them more than 600 years to stop the escalation of evil among them. But God would now deal with their evil by calling on the Israelites under Joshua to conquer them. The fertile land of Canaan would now set the scene for God to bless his people and let the surrounding nations know that he was the one true God who desired a relationship with all people.

GROUP DISCUSSION

Take a few minutes with your group members to discuss what you just watched and explore these concepts in Scripture.

1. What part of this week's teaching encouraged or challenged you the most? Why?

2. What does it mean to be "people of the Word"? How has knowing God's Word helped you to be courageous in the face of challenging situations?

3. What does it mean to be "people of prayer"? When are times that God provided you with courage and direction when you called out to him?

4. What does it mean to be "people identified with God"? What are some ways that you have shown that you truly belong to God and follow him?

5. What do you find most unsettling in the story of God instructing the Israelites to conquer the Canaanites and possess their land?

6. What is your biggest takeaway as you reflect on what you learned this week?

CLOSING PRAYER

End your group time by sharing prayer requests, reviewing how God has answered past prayers, and praying for one another. Use the space below to record any requests and praises. Also, make sure to pray for people God might add to your group—especially your neighbors.

Name   Request/Praise

FOR NEXT WEEK

Next week, we will look at how the Israelites failed to live up to God's standards when they entered into the Promised Land, the consequences that resulted, and how God continually rescued them. Before your next group meeting, be sure to read through the following personal study, complete the exercises, and memorize the key verse for the session.

VIDEO NOTES ANSWER KEY

overwhelming, 600 / Word / prayer, courageous / identified, belonging / Word, prayer, identified, successful / giants, giants

PERSONAL STUDY

Take some time after your group meeting this week to read through this section and complete the personal study. In total, it should take about one hour to complete. Allow the Scripture to take root in your heart as you review the story of the conquest of the Promised Land.

KNOW THE STORY

Nothing on the other side of the Jordan River had changed since Joshua and the other spies had first snuck in to check things out. If anything, the cities would have been even more heavily fortified. Forty years earlier, Joshua had been young and strong—maybe even a bit naive and impetuous. Now, older and wiser, he knew just how much the odds were stacked against him. His first major task would be to simply get the Israelites across the Jordan River. Only then would the real challenge begin—the conquest of the Promised Land.

After the death of Moses the servant of the LORD, the LORD said to Joshua son of Nun, Moses' aide: "Moses my servant is dead. Now then, you and all these people, get ready to cross the Jordan River into the land I am about to give to them—to the Israelites. I will give you every place where you set your foot, as I promised Moses. Your territory will extend from the desert to Lebanon, and from the great river, the Euphrates—

all the Hittite country—to the Mediterranean Sea in the west. No one will be able to stand against you all the days of your life. As I was with Moses, so I will be with you; I will never leave you nor forsake you. Be strong and courageous, because you will lead these people to inherit the land I swore to their ancestors to give them.

*"Be strong and very courageous. Be careful to obey all the law my servant Moses gave you; do not turn from it to the right or to the left, that you may be successful wherever you go. Keep this Book of the Law always on your lips; meditate on it day and night, so that you may be careful to do every-thing written in it. Then you will be prosperous and success-ful. Have I not commanded you? Be strong and courageous. Do not be afraid; do not be discouraged, for the L*ORD *your God will be with you wherever you go."*

*So Joshua ordered the officers of the people: "Go through the camp and tell the people, 'Get your provisions ready. Three days from now you will cross the Jordan here to go in and take possession of the land the L*ORD *your God is giving you for your own'"* (Joshua 1:1–10).

*Early in the morning Joshua and all the Israelites set out from Shittim and went to the Jordan, where they camped before crossing over. After three days the officers went throughout the camp, giving orders to the people: "When you see the ark of the covenant of the L*ORD *your God, and the Levitical priests carrying it, you are to move out from your positions and follow it. Then you will know which way to go, since you have never been this way before. But keep a distance of about two thousand cubits between you and the ark; do not go near it."*

Joshua told the people, "Consecrate yourselves, for tomorrow the LORD *will do amazing things among you."*

Joshua said to the priests, "Take up the ark of the covenant and pass on ahead of the people." So they took it up and went ahead of them. . . .

So when the people broke camp to cross the Jordan, the priests carrying the ark of the covenant went ahead of them. Now the Jordan is at flood stage all during harvest. Yet as soon as the priests who carried the ark reached the Jordan and their feet touched the water's edge, the water from upstream stopped flowing. It piled up in a heap a great distance away, at a town called Adam in the vicinity of Zarethan, while the water flowing down to the Sea of the Arabah (that is, the Dead Sea) was completely cut off. So the people crossed over opposite Jericho. The priests who carried the ark of the covenant of the LORD *stopped in the middle of the Jordan and stood on dry ground, while all Israel passed by until the whole nation had completed the crossing on dry ground.* (Joshua 3:1–6, 14–17).

Now the gates of Jericho were securely barred because of the Israelites. No one went out and no one came in.

Then the LORD *said to Joshua, "See, I have delivered Jericho into your hands, along with its king and its fighting men. March around the city once with all the armed men. Do this for six days. Have seven priests carry trumpets of rams' horns in front of the ark. On the seventh day, march around the city seven times, with the priests blowing the trumpets. When you hear them sound a long blast on the trumpets, have the whole army give a loud shout; then the wall of the city will collapse and the army will go up, everyone straight in." . . .*

On the seventh day, they got up at daybreak and marched around the city seven times in the same manner, except that on that day they circled the city seven times. The seventh time around, when the priests sounded the trumpet blast, Joshua commanded the army, "Shout! For the LORD has given you the city! The city and all that is in it are to be devoted to the LORD. Only Rahab the prostitute and all who are with her in her house shall be spared, because she hid the spies we sent. But keep away from the devoted things, so that you will not bring about your own destruction by taking any of them. Otherwise you will make the camp of Israel liable to destruction and bring trouble on it. All the silver and gold and the articles of bronze and iron are sacred to the LORD and must go into his treasury."

When the trumpets sounded, the army shouted, and at the sound of the trumpet, when the men gave a loud shout, the wall collapsed; so everyone charged straight in, and they took the city. They devoted the city to the Lord and destroyed with the sword every living thing in it—men and women, young and old, cattle, sheep and donkeys (Joshua 6:1–5, 15–21).

Then the five kings of the Amorites—the kings of Jerusalem, Hebron, Jarmuth, Lachish and Eglon—joined forces. They moved up with all their troops and took up positions against Gibeon and attacked it.

The Gibeonites then sent word to Joshua in the camp at Gilgal: "Do not abandon your servants. Come up to us quickly and save us! Help us, because all the Amorite kings from the hill country have joined forces against us."

So Joshua marched up from Gilgal with his entire army, including all the best fighting men. The LORD said to Joshua,

"Do not be afraid of them; I have given them into your hand. Not one of them will be able to withstand you."

After an all-night march from Gilgal, Joshua took them by surprise. The LORD *threw them into confusion before Israel, so Joshua and the Israelites defeated them completely at Gibeon. Israel pursued them along the road going up to Beth Horon and cut them down all the way to Azekah and Makkedah. As they fled before Israel on the road down from Beth Horon to Azekah, the* LORD *hurled large hailstones down on them, and more of them died from the hail than were killed by the swords of the Israelites* (Joshua 10:5–11).

So Joshua took this entire land: the hill country, all the Negev, the whole region of Goshen, the western foothills, the Arabah and the mountains of Israel with their foothills, from Mount Halak, which rises toward Seir, to Baal Gad in the Valley of Lebanon below Mount Hermon. He captured all their kings and put them to death. Joshua waged war against all these kings for a long time. Except for the Hivites living in Gibeon, not one city made a treaty of peace with the Israelites, who took them all in battle. For it was the LORD *himself who hardened their hearts to wage war against Israel, so that he might destroy them totally, exterminating them without mercy, as the* LORD *had commanded Moses.*

At that time Joshua went and destroyed the Anakites from the hill country: from Hebron, Debir and Anab, from all the hill country of Judah, and from all the hill country of Israel. Joshua totally destroyed them and their towns. No Anakites were left in Israelite territory; only in Gaza, Gath and Ashdod did any survive.

So Joshua took the entire land, just as the LORD had directed Moses, and he gave it as an inheritance to Israel according to their tribal divisions. Then the land had rest from war (Joshua 11:16–23).

1. What instructions did God give to Joshua as the Israelites prepared to enter the Promised Land?

2. How were the Israelites able to cross the Jordan River?

3. What were God's instructions the people for taking the city of Jericho?

4. How did God defeat the five kings of the Amorites on the Israelites' behalf?

_____

_____

_____

_____

5. Why did no city (except for Gibeon) try to make a treaty of peace with the Israelites?

_____

_____

_____

_____

UNDERSTAND THE STORY

Joshua must have experienced a sense of déjà vu as he stood on the borders of the Promised Land. He had been in this same place forty years before and watched as Israel had turned away from their inheritance. The challenge God had given them—to take the land—had not changed. But a transformation had taken place among the *people* of Israel. The former generation had passed away, and a new generation had arisen, ready to be led into the Promised Land.

Three key themes emerge as the Israelites enter this land of promise. First, it will be God's strength, not the strength of the Israelite army, that will make victory possible. In fact, the very first battle the people fight for Jericho is won with the sound of trumpets! Second, a heart of courage will be required on the part of the people. While the Lord promises to go before the Israelites, he still calls them to fight bravely. Third, if the Israelites were to have victory, they had to be people of God's word, people of prayer, and people identified with God.

Central to the conquest of Canaan is the concept of *fulfillment*. God was fulfilling the promise he made to Abraham some 600 years before to give the Promised Land to his descendants. But the Lord was also fulfilling his sentence of judgment against the Canaanite people, also spoken some 600 years earlier, when God declared that punishment of their sin was inevitable. The book of Joshua rings out clearly with this theme: *the Lord's way is the only way!*

1. What do the stories you have read this week tell you about God's promises?

2. How do these stories inspire you to take courageous risks for God?

LIVE THE STORY

Justice is served in a dramatic fashion when the Israelites capture the land and destroy its cities. But there is another reason as to why God gave this land to his people. He wanted to establish his name in Canaan so that everyone could know the one true God. He gave the land to the Israelites so that others would be drawn to this God who wants to be intimately involved with his people. The Lord continues to call us to be the kind of unique people who will attract others to him. And just like the Israelites, we will need courage if we are to live the way that God intends us to live. We must be *people of the Word* so that we know God's ways and can follow his guidelines. We must be *people of prayer* so we know when to move forward or hold our position. We must be *people identified with God* so others will be drawn to our loving Father.

1. How are others being attracted to God by the example you set in your life?

   _____

   _____

   _____

   _____

2. What is one action you will take this week to put what you've learned into practice?

   _____

   _____

   _____

TELL THE STORY

One day around a meal or your dinner table, have an intentional conversation about this week's topic with family or friends. During your time together, read Joshua 1:1–9, and then use the following question for discussion:

What are some ways that God might want you to show courage this week?

Ask God this week to help you fully embrace the story of Joshua and his courage. Also, spend a few minutes each day committing the key verse to memory: "Be strong and courageous. Do not be afraid; do not be discouraged, for the LORD your God will be with you wherever you go" (Joshua 1:9).

A FEW GOOD MEN . . . AND WOMEN

JUDGES 1–21

WELCOME

From a lower story perspective, it seemed that God's plan to create a new nation had again faltered. The Lord had brought the Israelites into the Promised Land. He had given them everything they needed to build a strong nation: guidelines on how to live, his presence in the tabernacle, and a way to atone for their sins. But the Israelites cannot stay focused on the upper story. Instead, they become addicted to worshiping the very gods the Lord had wanted them to stamp out. Such behavior results in God allowing other rulers to oppress them. This leads to a cycle of the Israelites recognizing their sin, calling out to God for help, and the Lord raising up a rescuer (called a "judge") to free them. During one of these periods, the Lord calls on a man who—like Moses before him—feels that he is not qualified for the job. But once again, God reveals that it is *his* power that matters . . . and not our own.

———— VIDEO TEACHING NOTES ————

Welcome to session seven of *God the Creator.* Spend a few minutes sharing any insights or questions about last week's personal study. Then watch the video (see the streaming video access provided on the inside front cover) The answer key is found at the end of the session.

- Israel has conquered the land under the leadership of _____, but as soon as Joshua dies, Israel turns from their full _____ to God. Why does Israel keep turning their back on God after all he has done for them?

- When the angel comes to visit Gideon, he is hiding in a _____ to thresh the wheat so the Midianites could not come and steal it. This has been going on for seven years, and Gideon is asking the "_____" question of the Lord.

- The truthful answer to the "why" question is simple: Israel is experiencing _____ from the surrounding pagan peoples because they did not keep up to their end of the Moses _____.

- Israel is massively _____ the identity of God and how beautiful life works when he is at the center of our lives. God forewarned them that he would be obligated to _____ them. This is why they are in the trouble they are in.

- As we have seen before with Abraham and Moses, God often selects the most _____ candidate to accomplish his upper story plan. Why? So that when it is _____, everyone will know it was God and turn to him.

- We get ourselves into all sorts of trouble because we want to live life our way, not God's way. We think in the lower story that God has _____ us. But in the upper story, God is waiting for us to _____ to him.

GETTING STARTED

Begin your discussion by reciting the key verses and key idea together as a group. Now try to state the key verses from memory. On your first attempt, use your notes if you need help. On your second attempt, try to state it completely from memory.

Key Verses: "I delivered you from the hand of all your oppressors; I drove them out before you and gave you their land. "I said to you, 'I am the LORD your God; do not worship the gods of the Amorites, in whose land you live.' But you have not listened to me" (Judges 6:9–10).

KEY IDEA: God continues to accomplish his mission of redemption by giving the land of Canaan to the Israelites. However, once there, the people repeatedly sin against him, resulting in God allowing them to fall captive to other nations. When the people repent, God raises up judges to free them. He continues to rescue them because he made an unconditional promise that the solution for all people to come back into a relationship with him would come through Israel.

GROUP DISCUSSION

Take a few minutes with your group members to discuss what you just watched and explore these concepts in Scripture.

1. What part of this week's teaching encouraged or challenged you the most? Why?

2. What question did Gideon ask when the angel said that the Lord was with him? What caused Gideon to ask this particular question?

3. How did God reveal that Gideon was a "mighty warrior"—but not in his own strength?

4. When are some times that you have felt abandoned by God?

5. What does the story of Gideon reveal about God's continual presence in your life?

6. What is your biggest takeaway as you reflect on what you learned this week?

CLOSING PRAYER

End your group time by sharing prayer requests, reviewing how God has answered past prayers, and praying for one another. Use the space below to record any requests and praises. Also, make sure to pray for people God might add to your group—especially your neighbors.

Name   Request/Praise

_____   _____

_____   _____

_____   _____

_____   _____

_____   _____

_____   _____

FOR NEXT WEEK

Next week, we will look at the story of Ruth and how the Lord used her faithfulness and character to continue his upper story through the lineage of Jesus. Before your next group meeting, be sure to read through the following personal study, complete the exercises, and memorize the key verses for the session.

VIDEO NOTES ANSWER KEY

Joshua, devotion / winepress, why / oppression, covenant / distorting, discipline / unlikely, accomplished / abandoned / return

PERSONAL STUDY

Take some time after your group meeting this week to read through this section and complete the personal study. In total, it should take about one hour to complete. Allow the Scripture to take root in your heart and ask God to give you insights into the story of Gideon.

KNOW THE STORY

If the story of God's people in the book of Joshua demonstrates what the Israelites did right, then their story in the book of Judges shows what they did wrong. A popular definition of insanity is doing the same thing again and again yet expecting different results. If that is true, then God's people at this time were trapped in madness, living in a cycle of disobedience, crying out to God for help and falling back into patterns of idolatry and sin. As story after story is recounted, a clear "sin cycle," emerges. God's people are perpetually spinning through stages of sin, oppression, repentance, and deliverance . . . from one generation to the next.

> *After the death of Joshua, the Israelites asked the LORD, "Who of us is to go up first to fight against the Canaanites?"*
> *The LORD answered, "Judah shall go up; I have given the land into their hands."*

The men of Judah then said to the Simeonites their fellow Israelites, "Come up with us into the territory allotted to us, to fight against the Canaanites. We in turn will go with you into yours." So the Simeonites went with them.

When Judah attacked, the LORD gave the Canaanites and Perizzites into their hands, and they struck down ten thousand men at Bezek. . . .

The LORD was with the men of Judah. They took possession of the hill country, but they were unable to drive the people from the plains, because they had chariots fitted with iron. As Moses had promised, Hebron was given to Caleb, who drove from it the three sons of Anak. The Benjamites, however, did not drive out the Jebusites, who were living in Jerusalem; to this day the Jebusites live there with the Benjamites.

Now the tribes of Joseph attacked Bethel, and the LORD was with them. When they sent men to spy out Bethel (formerly called Luz), the spies saw a man coming out of the city and they said to him, "Show us how to get into the city and we will see that you are treated well." So he showed them, and they put the city to the sword but spared the man and his whole family. He then went to the land of the Hittites, where he built a city and called it Luz, which is its name to this day (Judges 1:1–4, 19–26).

Joshua son of Nun, the servant of the Lord, died at the age of a hundred and ten. And they buried him in the land of his inheritance, at Timnath Heres in the hill country of Ephraim, north of Mount Gaash.

After that whole generation had been gathered to their ancestors, another generation grew up who knew neither the

LORD nor what he had done for Israel. Then the Israelites did evil in the eyes of the LORD and served the Baals. They forsook the LORD, the God of their ancestors, who had brought them out of Egypt. They followed and worshiped various gods of the peoples around them. They aroused the LORD's anger because they forsook him and served Baal and the Ashtoreths. In his anger against Israel the LORD gave them into the hands of raiders who plundered them. He sold them into the hands of their enemies all around, whom they were no longer able to resist. Whenever Israel went out to fight, the hand of the LORD was against them to defeat them, just as he had sworn to them. They were in great distress.

Then the LORD raised up judges, who saved them out of the hands of these raiders. Yet they would not listen to their judges but prostituted themselves to other gods and worshiped them. They quickly turned from the ways of their ancestors, who had been obedient to the LORD's commands. Whenever the LORD raised up a judge for them, he was with the judge and saved them out of the hands of their enemies as long as the judge lived; for the LORD relented because of their groaning under those who oppressed and afflicted them. But when the judge died, the people returned to ways even more corrupt than those of their ancestors, following other gods and serving and worshiping them. They refused to give up their evil practices and stubborn ways (Judges 2:8–19).

The angel of the LORD came and sat down under the oak in Ophrah that belonged to Joash the Abiezrite, where his son Gideon was threshing wheat in a winepress to keep it from the Midianites. When the angel of the LORD appeared to Gideon, he said, "The LORD is with you, mighty warrior."

"Pardon me, my lord," Gideon replied, *"but if the LORD is with us, why has all this happened to us? Where are all his wonders that our ancestors told us about when they said, 'Did not the LORD bring us up out of Egypt?' But now the LORD has abandoned us and given us into the hand of Midian."*

The LORD turned to him and said, "Go in the strength you have and save Israel out of Midian's hand. Am I not sending you?"

"Pardon me, my lord," Gideon replied, *"but how can I save Israel? My clan is the weakest in Manasseh, and I am the least in my family."*

The LORD answered, "I will be with you, and you will strike down all the Midianites, leaving none alive" (Judges 6:11–16).

Early in the morning, Jerub-Baal (that is, Gideon) and all his men camped at the spring of Harod. The camp of Midian was north of them in the valley near the hill of Moreh. The LORD said to Gideon, "You have too many men. I cannot deliver Midian into their hands, or Israel would boast against me, 'My own strength has saved me.' Now announce to the army, 'Anyone who trembles with fear may turn back and leave Mount Gilead.'" So twenty-two thousand men left, while ten thousand remained.

But the LORD said to Gideon, "There are still too many men. Take them down to the water, and I will thin them out for you there. If I say, 'This one shall go with you,' he shall go; but if I say, 'This one shall not go with you,' he shall not go."

So Gideon took the men down to the water. There the Lord told him, "Separate those who lap the water with their tongues as a dog laps from those who kneel down to drink." Three hundred of them drank from cupped hands, lapping like dogs. All the rest got down on their knees to drink.

The LORD said to Gideon, "With the three hundred men that lapped I will save you and give the Midianites into your hands. Let all the others go home." So Gideon sent the rest of the Israelites home but kept the three hundred, who took over the provisions and trumpets of the others. . . .

Gideon and the hundred men with him reached the edge of the camp at the beginning of the middle watch, just after they had changed the guard. They blew their trumpets and broke the jars that were in their hands. The three companies blew the trumpets and smashed the jars. Grasping the torches in their left hands and holding in their right hands the trumpets they were to blow, they shouted, "A sword for the LORD and for Gideon!" While each man held his position around the camp, all the Midianites ran, crying out as they fled.

When the three hundred trumpets sounded, the LORD caused the men throughout the camp to turn on each other with their swords. The army fled to Beth Shittah toward Zererah as far as the border of Abel Meholah near Tabbath. Israelites from Naphtali, Asher and all Manasseh were called out, and they pursued the Midianites. Gideon sent messengers throughout the hill country of Ephraim, saying, "Come down against the Midianites and seize the waters of the Jordan ahead of them as far as Beth Barah."

So all the men of Ephraim were called out and they seized the waters of the Jordan as far as Beth Barah. They also captured two of the Midianite leaders, Oreb and Zeeb. They killed Oreb at the rock of Oreb, and Zeeb at the winepress of Zeeb. They pursued the Midianites and brought the heads of

Oreb and Zeeb to Gideon, who was by the Jordan (Judges 7:1–8, 19–25).

1. What successes did the Israelites have immediately after the death of Joshua?

   _____

   _____

   _____

   _____

2. What happened after that generation had passed to the Israelites living in Canaan?

   _____

   _____

   _____

   _____

3. What was Gideon doing when the angel of the Lord appeared to him?

   _____

   _____

   _____

   _____

4. Why did God ask Gideon to dismiss all but 300 men in his army?

   _____

   _____

   _____

   _____

5. How did the Lord deliver the Midianites into Gideon's hands?

_____

_____

_____

_____

UNDERSTAND THE STORY

The Lord had called the people of Israel out of the nations to have a distinct voice and presence in the world. But increasingly, the Israelites looked no different from the world around them. From one generation to the next, the people forgot the Lord. They neglected the clear command that Moses had given to them: "These commandments that I give you today are to be on your hearts. Impress them on your children. Talk about them when you sit at home and when you walk along the road, when you lie down and when you get up" (Deuteronomy 6:6–7).

The Israelites forgot that they had been called to be a distinctive and holy people in an unholy culture. They had won the land of promise . . . but lost the war against complacency. As a result, the Lord executed his hand of judgment against them. He had to make the people's circumstances dire enough so they would awaken to just how far they had drifted away from him. But the overarching theme of the story of Judges is that God did not just leave them there. Even when they were faithless to him, he was ever faithful to them.

As Christians, we get ourselves into all sorts of trouble because we—like the Israelites—want to live life the way we want instead of the way that God wants. When we do this, we will suffer the consequences of our actions . . . and we may fear that God has abandoned us because of the depth of our sin against him. But the reality is that God is always waiting for us to return to him when we stray. Like the loving Father he is, he opens his arms and says, "I will take you back. Always. No matter what you've done. I will deliver you because I love you."

1. What do the stories you have read this week reveal about God's faithfulness to you . . . even when you are not always faithful to him?

_____

_____

_____

_____

2. How will these stories help you to understand the consequences of sin?

_____

_____

_____

_____

LIVE THE STORY

If you've ever felt outnumbered, unqualified, or disadvantaged, you can be encouraged by Gideon's story. When he first appears in Judges, he is a deeply flawed individual who struggles with fear and is inclined toward disobedience to God's commands. He has a difficult time believing that God would actually choose *him* to save Israel. He "reminds" God that he is from the weakest tribe in Israel and that he is the youngest in his family . . . not exactly gladiator material. Yet the Lord works with this reluctant hero to get the job done. By the end of Gideon's story, we find that he did at least one thing exactly right: *he kept walking forward into God's will.* Just that little bit of faith was all that God needed to craft him into a mighty warrior. In the same way, he will use each of us as we step forward with even a little bit of faith.

1. What is one small step of faith that God is asking you to take today?

   _____

   _____

   _____

2. What is one action you will take this week to put what you've learned into practice?

   _____

   _____

   _____

TELL THE STORY

One day around a meal or your dinner table, have an intentional conversation about this week's topic with family or friends. During your time together, read Judges 6:1–16, and then use the following question for discussion:

What are different ways God can use small things and young people to help bless the world around us?

Ask God this week to help you fully embrace the story of Gideon's growing trust in God. Also, spend a few minutes each day committing the key verses to memory: "I delivered you from the hand of all your oppressors; I drove them out before you and gave you their land. "I said to you, 'I am the LORD your God; do not worship the gods of the Amorites, in whose land you live.' But you have not listened to me" (Judges 6:9–10).

THE FAITH OF A FOREIGN WOMAN

RUTH 1–4

WELCOME

Every time a couple decides to watch a movie together, they are faced with a decision: *action or romance film?* God's Story certainly has its share of action. Abraham is asked to sacrifice Isaac. Joseph endures scorn, abuse, and prison to ultimately rise up as the hero. God calls down ten plagues against Egypt. Joshua leads his hearty band of followers against powerful foes in Canaan. God delivers his people time and again when they repent. So it's surprising to find that right in the heart of all this action—during the period of the judges—the Bible takes a break to highlight a romance story. At the lower-story level, it is a simple plot of two people from different backgrounds finding love. But at the upper-story level, a greater plot is unfolding . . . a story of how God is continuing to use unlikely characters to execute his plan.

VIDEO TEACHING NOTES

Welcome to session eight of *God the Creator*. Spend a few minutes sharing any insights or questions about last week's personal study. Then watch the video (see the streaming video access provided on the inside front cover) The answer key is found at the end of the session.

- In the lower story all _____ is lost for Naomi. She moved from Bethlehem to Moab with her husband to weather the storm of a _____ in the land. Not long after they arrive, her husband dies.

- Ruth is a _____. The Moabites had oppressed the Israelites for eighteen years before Ehud the judge delivered them. In the lower story there was little chance she would be _____, yet this is the path she chose.

- A concept taught in the law stated that if a man died without an ___, the next of kin had the option to marry his widow, care for her, pay off her financial debts, and redeem the land. This man is called the "_____."

- Ruth was asking Boaz to be God's _____ to her—and he accepted. He not only bought Ruth's widow's land but all his brother's land and Elimelech's land as well. He risked his own estate and _____ them all.

- Ruth and Boaz had a little _____ together. The little one didn't know it yet, but he would inherit the land of his "father" Mahlon whom he never met. He will carry out the _____ _____ because of the kind act of Boaz.

- God was not only _____ above the scene of Ruth's life to provide for her earthly needs in the lower story, but he was also _____ out his upper story plan with her in mind. He went out of his way to include an outsider, a pagan Moabite, in the lineage of _____. This is extreme acceptance!

GETTING STARTED

Begin your discussion by reciting the key verse and key idea together as a group. Now try to state the key verse from memory. On your first attempt, use your notes if you need help. On your second attempt, try to state it completely from memory.

KEY VERSE: "Don't urge me to leave you or to turn back from you. Where you go I will go, and where you stay I will stay. Your people will be my people and your God my God" (Ruth 1:16).

KEY IDEA: During the period of the judges, a couple and their two sons move from Bethlehem to Moab during a time of famine. The husband soon dies, leaving the woman—named Naomi—a widow. In time, her sons marry Moabite women, one of whom is named Ruth. When both sons die, Naomi decides to return to Bethlehem, and Ruth declares allegiance to her God. Once there, Ruth marries a relative named Boaz. Ruth and Boaz have a son who will become the grandfather of King David in the direct lineage of Jesus.

GROUP DISCUSSION

Take a few minutes with your group members to discuss what you just watched and explore these concepts in Scripture.

1. What part of this week's teaching encouraged or challenged you the most? Why?

2. Why did Naomi ask the women of Bethlehem to call her "Mara," which means bitter?

3. How did God orchestrate the events that led to Boaz marrying Ruth and agreeing to take on the role of the family's kinsman redeemer?

4. What does the story of Ruth and Boaz tell you about the kinds of people that God chooses to include in his greater plans?

5. What greater upper-story plot is revealed at the end of this simple love story?

6. What is your biggest takeaway as you reflect on what you learned this week?

CLOSING PRAYER

End your group time by sharing prayer requests, reviewing how God has answered past prayers, and praying for one another. Use the space below to record any requests and praises. Also, make sure to pray for people God might add to your group—especially your neighbors.

Name   Request/Praise

_____   _____

_____   _____

_____   _____

_____   _____

_____   _____

_____   _____

_____   _____

IN THE COMING DAYS

In the days ahead, be sure to read through the following personal study, complete the exercises, and memorize the key verses for the session.

VIDEO NOTES ANSWER KEY

hope, famine / Moabite, accepted / heir, kinsman redeemer / wing, redeemed / boy, family name / working, working, Jesus

PERSONAL STUDY

Take some time after your group meeting this week to read through this section and complete the personal study. In total, it should take about one hour to complete. Allow the Scripture to take root in your heart as you review the story of Naomi, Boaz, and Ruth.

KNOW THE STORY

This curious account of an Israelite widow and her Moabite daughter-in-law highlights that God's saving purpose is not for Israel alone. Ruth, a Moabite woman, came from a pagan culture that represented a constant threat to the Israelites. Yet God would use Ruth's loyalty and faith in his upper story to ultimately redeem people through her descendant—Jesus.

In the days when the judges ruled, there was a famine in the land. So a man from Bethlehem in Judah, together with his wife and two sons, went to live for a while in the country of Moab. The man's name was Elimelek, his wife's name was Naomi, and the names of his two sons were Mahlon and Kilion. They were Ephrathites from Bethlehem, Judah. And they went to Moab and lived there.

Now Elimelek, Naomi's husband, died, and she was left with her two sons. They married Moabite women, one named Orpah and the other Ruth. After they had lived there

*about ten years, both Mahlon and Kilion also died, and
Naomi was left without her two sons and her husband.*

*When Naomi heard in Moab that the Lord had come to
the aid of his people by providing food for them, she and her
daughters-in-law prepared to return home from there. With
her two daughters-in-law she left the place where she had
been living and set out on the road that would take them back
to the land of Judah.*

*Then Naomi said to her two daughters-in-law, "Go
back, each of you, to your mother's home. May the Lord
show you kindness, as you have shown kindness to your dead
husbands and to me. May the Lord grant that each of you
will find rest in the home of another husband.". . .*

*But Ruth replied, "Don't urge me to leave you or to turn
back from you. Where you go I will go, and where you stay
I will stay. Your people will be my people and your God
my God. Where you die I will die, and there I will be buried.
May the Lord deal with me, be it ever so severely, if even
death separates you and me." When Naomi realized that
Ruth was determined to go with her, she stopped urging her*
(Ruth 1:1–9, 16–18).

*Now Naomi had a relative on her husband's side, a man of
standing from the clan of Elimelek, whose name was Boaz.*

*And Ruth the Moabite said to Naomi, "Let me go to the
fields and pick up the leftover grain behind anyone in whose
eyes I find favor."*

*Naomi said to her, "Go ahead, my daughter." So she
went out, entered a field and began to glean behind the har-
vesters. As it turned out, she was working in a field belonging
to Boaz, who was from the clan of Elimelek. . . .*

So Boaz said to Ruth, "My daughter, listen to me. Don't go and glean in another field and don't go away from here. Stay here with the women who work for me. Watch the field where the men are harvesting, and follow along after the women. I have told the men not to lay a hand on you. And whenever you are thirsty, go and get a drink from the water jars the men have filled." . . .

Then Ruth told her mother-in-law about the one at whose place she had been working. "The name of the man I worked with today is Boaz," she said.

"The Lord *bless him!" Naomi said to her daughter-in-law. "He has not stopped showing his kindness to the living and the dead." She added, "That man is our close relative; he is one of our guardian-redeemers"* (Ruth 2:1–3, 8–9, 19–20).

One day Ruth's mother-in-law Naomi said to her, "My daughter, I must find a home for you, where you will be well provided for. Now Boaz, with whose women you have worked, is a relative of ours. Tonight he will be winnowing barley on the threshing floor. Wash, put on perfume, and get dressed in your best clothes. Then go down to the threshing floor, but don't let him know you are there until he has finished eating and drinking. When he lies down, note the place where he is lying. Then go and uncover his feet and lie down. He will tell you what to do."

"I will do whatever you say," Ruth answered. So she went down to the threshing floor and did everything her mother-in-law told her to do.

When Boaz had finished eating and drinking and was in good spirits, he went over to lie down at the far end of the grain pile. Ruth approached quietly, uncovered his feet and lay down. In the middle of the night something startled the man; he turned—and there was a woman lying at his feet!

"Who are you?" he asked.

"I am your servant Ruth," she said. "Spread the corner of your garment over me, since you are a guardian-redeemer of our family" (Ruth 3:1–9).

Then Boaz announced to the elders and all the people, "Today you are witnesses that I have bought from Naomi all the property of Elimelek, Kilion and Mahlon. I have also acquired Ruth the Moabite, Mahlon's widow, as my wife, in order to maintain the name of the dead with his property, so that his name will not disappear from among his family or from his hometown. Today you are witnesses!"

Then the elders and all the people at the gate said, "We are witnesses. May the LORD make the woman who is coming into your home like Rachel and Leah, who together built up the family of Israel. May you have standing in Ephrathah and be famous in Bethlehem. Through the offspring the LORD gives you by this young woman, may your family be like that of Perez, whom Tamar bore to Judah."

So Boaz took Ruth and she became his wife. When he made love to her, the LORD enabled her to conceive, and she gave birth to a son. The women said to Naomi: "Praise be to the LORD, who this day has not left you without a guardian-redeemer. May he become famous throughout Israel! He will renew your life and sustain you in your old age. For your daughter-in-law, who loves you and who is better to you than seven sons, has given him birth" (Ruth 4:9–15).

1. What tragic events led to Naomi deciding to return to Bethlehem?

2. How did Ruth respond when Naomi told her to go back to Moab?

3. How did Boaz react when he saw Ruth gleaning in his fields?

4. What was Naomi's strategy to "find a home" for Ruth?

5. What did Boaz pronounce at the end of the story to the elders in Bethlehem?

_____

_____

_____

_____

UNDERSTAND THE STORY

Key to understanding the story of Ruth is understanding the role of the "kinsman-redeemer," or *go'el*. In a tribal culture like Israel, family members were expected to take care of relatives. When the male in a household died, his next of kin (also a male) played an especially important role. In particular, he could be called upon by the family to fulfill three specific duties.

First, to *redeem property and/or relatives*. In Israel, all property was a family possession. If land or a relative was sold to pay off debt, it was the kinsman-redeemer's duty to pay off that debt, thereby redeeming the land or relative. Second, *to provide an heir through marriage*. If a man died without an heir, it was the surviving brother's duty to marry the widow and provide an heir to carry on his brother's name and maintain his inheritance. Third, *to avenge the unlawful death of a family member*. The *go'el haddam*, or "avenger of blood," served a legal function in Israel, pursuing and executing justice on anyone who killed a family member.

Boaz sought to fulfill the role of kinsman-redeemer for Ruth not simply out of obligation (a closer kinsman was obligated to do that) but out of love. He had seen her faithful support of Naomi, watched her operate with integrity, and felt privileged to find such a woman. In the process, Boaz in the lower story points us to Jesus in the upper story, who will come later to serve as our Guardian-Redeemer. He will redeem all who want his wings of forgiveness to cover them . . . even outsiders. After all, Jesus came from the family of an outsider named Ruth!

1. What do the stories you have read this week reveal about the price God was willing to pay to become your "kinsman-redeemer"?

2. How do these stories help you to understand how God can redeem your story?

LIVE THE STORY

In the lower story, Naomi thought her life was over. After the death of a husband and two sons, she believed that God had abandoned her and that her life would be nothing but bitterness. But God was working on her behalf in the upper story. He provided for her and turned her despair into hope through the birth of Ruth and Boaz's son. The little boy was named Obed, which means "worker." Naomi had been forced to sell her family's land because she was unable to work it, but God had provided the worker needed to redeem it. Our story at times may seem likewise hopeless and bitter to the taste. But we can be sure that God is *working* on our behalf in the upper story—redeeming our story and working things out for our good.

1. What are some ways you have seen God working on your behalf—in spite of any times of bitterness or hardship that you have faced?

   _____

   _____

   _____

   _____

2. What is one action you will take this week to put what you've learned into practice?

   _____

   _____

   _____

   _____

TELL THE STORY

One day around a meal or your dinner table, have an intentional conversation about this week's topic with family or friends. During your time together, read Ruth 1:1–22, and then use the following question for discussion:

Who are some of the people God has brought into your life to help you during difficult times?

Ask God this week to help you fully embrace the story of Ruth. Also, spend a few minutes each day committing the key verse to memory: "Don't urge me to leave you or to turn back from you. Where you go I will go, and where you stay I will stay. Your people will be my people and your God my God" (Ruth 1:16).

LEADER'S GUIDE

Thank you for your willingness to lead your group through this study! What you have chosen to do is valuable and will make a great difference in the lives of others. The rewards of being a leader are different from those participating, and we hope that as you lead you will find your own walk with Jesus deepened by this experience.

God the Creator is an eight-session study in *The Story* series built around video content and small-group interaction. As the group leader, just think of yourself as the host of a dinner party. Your job is to take care of your guests by managing all the behind-the-scenes details so that when everyone arrives, they can just enjoy time together.

As the group leader, your role is not to answer all the questions or reteach the content—the video and study guide will do most of that work. Your job is to guide the experience and cultivate your small group into a kind of teaching community. This will make it a place for members to process, question, and reflect—not receive more instruction.

Before your first meeting, make sure the group members have a copy of the study guide. Also make sure they are aware that they have access to the videos at any time through the streaming code provided on the inside front cover. This will keep everyone on the same page and help the process run more smoothly. If some members are unable to purchase the guide, arrange it so they can share the resource with other group members. Giving everyone access to all the material will position this study to be as rewarding an experience as possible. Everyone should feel free to write in his or her study guide and bring it to group every week.

SETTING UP THE GROUP

You will need to determine with your group how long you want to meet each week so that you can plan your time accordingly. Generally, most groups like to meet for either ninety minutes or two hours, so you could use one of the following schedules:

SECTION	90 MINUTES	120 MINUTES
WELCOME (members arrive and get settled)	15 minutes	15 minutes
WATCH (watch the teaching material together and take notes)	15 minutes	15 minutes
DISCUSS (recite the key verse and key idea and discuss study questions you selected)	40 minutes	60 minutes
PRAY (close your time in prayer)	20 minutes	30 minutes

As the group leader, you will want to create an environment that encourages sharing and learning. A church sanctuary or formal classroom may not be as ideal as a living room in this regard, because those locations can feel formal and less intimate. No matter what setting you choose, provide enough comfortable seating for everyone, and, if possible, arrange the seats in a semicircle so everyone can see the video easily. This will make transition between the video and group conversation more efficient and natural.

If you are meeting in person, get to the meeting site early so you can greet participants as they arrive. Simple refreshments create a welcoming atmosphere and can be a wonderful addition to a group study evening. Be sure to take food and pet allergies into account to make your guests as comfortable as possible. You may also want to consider offering childcare to couples with children who want to attend. Finally, be sure your media technology is working properly. Managing these details up front will make the rest of your group experience flow smoothly and provide a welcoming space to engage the content of *God the Creator*.

STRUCTURING THE GROUP TIME

Once everyone has arrived, it's time to begin the group. Here are some simple tips to make your group time healthy, enjoyable, and effective.

First, begin the meeting with a short prayer and remind the group members to put their phones on silent. This is a way to make sure you can all be present with one another and with God. Next, watch the video and instruct the participants to follow along in their guides and take notes. After the video teaching, have the group recite the key verse and key idea together before moving on to the discussion questions.

Encourage all the group members to participate in the discussion, but make sure they know they don't have to do so.

As the discussion progresses, you may want to follow up with comments such as, "Tell me more about that," or, "Why did you answer that way?" This will allow the group participants to deepen their reflections and invite meaningful sharing in a nonthreatening way.

Note that you have been given multiple questions to use in each session, and you do not have to use them all or even follow them in order. Feel free to pick and choose questions based on either the needs of your group or how the conversation is flowing. Also, don't be afraid of silence. Offering a question and allowing up to thirty seconds of silence is okay. It allows people space to think about how they want to respond and also gives them time to do so.

As group leader, you are the boundary keeper for your group. Do not let anyone (yourself included) dominate the group time. Keep an eye out for group members who might be tempted to "attack" folks they disagree with or try to "fix" those having struggles. These kinds of behaviors can derail a group's momentum, so they need to be steered in a different direction. Model active listening and encourage everyone in your group to do the same. This will make your group time a safe space and create a positive community.

CONCLUDING THE GROUP TIME

At the conclusion of session one, invite the group members to complete the between-sessions personal studies for that week. Also let them know that if they choose to do so, they can watch the video for the following week by accessing the streaming code found on the inside front cover of their studies. Explain that you will be providing some time before the video teaching the following week for anyone to share any insights. (Do this as part of the opening "Welcome" beginning in session two, right before you watch the video.) Let them know sharing is optional.

Thank you again for taking the time to lead your group and helping them to understand the greater story of the Bible in *God the Creator*. You are making a difference in the lives of others and having an impact for the kingdom of God!

God the Deliverer

Our Search for Identity and Our Hope for Renewal

Study Guide
9780310134787

DVD with
Free Streaming Access
9780310134800

This study will introduce you to the lower and upper stories as told in the Old Testament books of 1 Samuel through Malachi to explore how God's plan was at work through the exile and restoration of Israel. As you read these narratives—featuring characters such as Samuel, Saul, David, Jeremiah, Daniel, Esther, Ezra, and Nehemiah—you will see how God has been weaving our lower story into the greater upper story that he has been writing.

Churches can embrace THE STORY for a full ministry year through worship services, small group studies, and family activities.
Learn more about this whole-church experience at TheStory.com.

God the Savior

Our Freedom in Christ and Our Role in the Restoration of All Things

Study Guide
9780310134930

DVD with
Free Streaming Access
9780310134954

This study reveals how God's upper-story plan ultimately came to fulfillment through the birth, ministry, death, and resurrection of Christ. In the New Testament, you will read these stories—featuring characters such as Mary and Joseph, the Twelve Disciples, John the Baptist, Mary Magdalene, the Apostle Paul, and the central figure Jesus Christ—discovering how God has been weaving our lower story into the greater upper story that he has been writing.

HarperChristianResources

THE STORY

POWERED BY ZONDERVAN

READ THE STORY. EXPERIENCE THE BIBLE.

Here I am, 50 years old. I have been to college, seminary, engaged in ministry my whole life, my dad is in ministry, my grandfather was in ministry, and **The Story has been one of the most unique experiences of my life**. The Bible has been made fresh for me. It has made God's redemptive plan come alive for me once again.
—Seth Buckley, Youth Pastor, Spartanburg Baptist Church, Spartanburg, SC

We have people reading *The Story*—some devour it **and can't wait for the next week**. Some have never really read the Bible much, so it's exciting to see a lot of adults reading the Word of God for the first time. I've heard wonderful things from people who are long-time readers of Scripture. They're excited about how it's all being tied together for them. It just seems to make more sense.
—Lynnette Schulz, Director of Worship Peace Lutheran Church, Eau Claire, WI

As my family and I went through *The Story* together, the more I began to believe and the more real [the Bible] became to me, and **it rubbed off on my children and helped them with their walk with the Lord**. *The Story* inspired conversations we might not normally have had.
—Kelly Leonard, Parent, Shepherd of the Hills Christian Church, Porter Ranch, CA

FOR ADULTS

9780310458197

FOR TEENS

9780310458463

FOR KIDS

9780310719250

TheStory.com

The Life-Changing
Bible Engagement Experience
That Will
Transform
Your Church

Impactful, proven, trusted, and easy to implement, THE STORY is the gold-standard Bible engagement program for whole churches.

THE STORY

With curriculum and books for all ages, along with preaching resources, small group study, youth group activities, and parent helps, *The Story Church Resource Kit* is your complete resource for the entire ministry year.

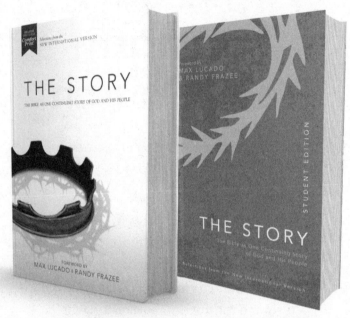

If You Want to Grow in Your Faith, You Must Engage God's Word

What you believe in your heart will define who you become. God wants you to become like Jesus—it is the most truthful and powerful way to live—and the journey to becoming like Jesus begins by thinking like Jesus.

Jesus compared the Christian life to a vine. He is the vine; you are the branches. If you remain in the vine of Christ, over time you will produce amazing and scrumptious fruit for all to see and taste. You begin to act like Jesus, and become more like Jesus.

In the **Believe Bible Study Series**, bestselling author and pastor Randy Frazee helps you ask three big questions:

- What do I believe and why does it matter?
- How can I put my faith into action?
- Am I becoming the person God wants me to be?

Each of the three eight-session studies in this series include video teaching from Randy Frazee and a study guide with video study notes, group discussion questions, Scripture reading, and activities for personal growth and reflection.

As you journey through this study series, whether in a group or on your own, one simple truth will become undeniably clear: what you believe drives everything.

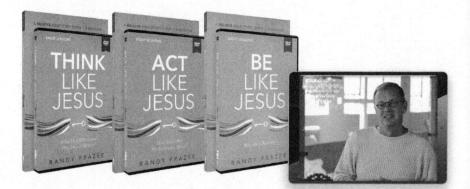

Available now at your favorite bookstore, or streaming video on StudyGateway.com.